Choosing a
Catholic School

A practical guide

C000280882

CONTENTS

Foreword by Archbishop Malcolm McMahon OP — Page 3

Introduction — Page 4

Part I

Chapter 1 — *What should I look for and how do I get my child into a Catholic school?* — Page 10

Chapter 2 — *Parent views* — Page 24

Chapter 3 — *Pupils getting ready – what your child needs to know* — Page 36

Chapter 4 — *What difference has being in a Catholic school made to us?* — Page 54

Chapter 5 — *Will a Catholic education help my child in the world of work?* — Page 66

Chapter 6 — *Expectations of parents and carers of children in Catholic schools* — Page 78

Part II

Chapter 7 — *What does the Catholic Church say about education?* — Page 88

Chapter 8 — *Who is responsible for a Catholic school?* — Page 102

Appendix — *Key documents concerning worldwide Catholic education* — Page 112

FOREWORD

I am very pleased to be able say a word at the beginning of this very helpful work by Sister Judith Russi.

The bishops of England and Wales as long ago as 1852 gave priority to building schools for Catholic children, and they continue in this mission today. Catholic schools provide a full education with Christ at its centre, within the context of the wider community of the Church. Over many decades the Catholic school system has developed to meet these aims in partnership with the State. Quite rightly, the Catholic Church is very proud of its schools.

Nevertheless the Church recognises the important responsibility that parents have for their children's education. The Second Vatican Council declared that "The role of parents in education is of such importance that it is almost impossible to provide an adequate substitute" (*Gravissimum Educationis*, Declaration on Christian Education, 3). But the Church has a part to play too, and that is to support parents in this great adventure of their children's education. As the bishop with responsibility for the Catholic Education Service as well as my own diocese, I understand the complexity of the decision that parents have to make when choosing a school for their child.

Jesus tells us, "I have come that they may have life, life in all its fullness" (John 10:10). I believe that a Catholic education is a valuable stage on that journey to the fullness of life, and I am sure that Sister Judith's book will guide many parents towards making good decisions regarding their children's future.

+ Malcolm Mc Mahon op

Archbishop Malcolm McMahon OP
Chair of the Catholic Education Service

INTRODUCTION

I hope this book will be a helpful resource as you face the big decision about which school to send your child to and the complexities of the admissions process.

For those who have already decided on the school and have a place then hopefully you will find it a useful tool for the ongoing support of your child throughout his or her schooling.

Demand for places in a Catholic school is often very high. This is not surprising as Catholic schools have an impressive reputation and are therefore very popular. Contrary to the image sometimes portrayed in the media about what are termed "faith schools", standards in Catholic schools are generally higher than those in schools of no particular faith background in almost every Ofsted (Office for Standards in Education, Children's Services and Skills) category.

Every year Ofsted publishes statistics about the performance of schools nationally. The following is an overview of the latest data for 2015. You can read the full report drawn up by Catholic Education Service at **www.catholiceducation.org.uk/ces-census**. These reports come out each year so you can always access the latest information.

How many Catholic schools are there?

There are 2,142 Catholic schools in England. Catholic schools make up 10% of the national total of maintained schools.

How are they made up?

819,069 pupils are educated in Catholic schools.

69% of pupils at Catholic maintained schools are Catholic.

46,479 teachers work in Catholic maintained schools.

53% of teachers in Catholic maintained schools are Catholic.

What about academic standards?

At age eleven, Catholic schools outperform the national average English and Maths SATs scores by 6%.

83% of Catholic secondary schools have Ofsted grades of good or outstanding (75% nationally).

At GCSE, Catholic schools outperform the national average by 5%.

Clearly we can see that academic standards are higher at the end of both primary and secondary education.

Are they inclusive?

It is interesting to see that Catholic schools are the most culturally diverse in the country and fully inclusive. This is no surprise because by its very nature the Catholic community is a global community. This is clearly evidenced in our schools.

37% of pupils in Catholic maintained primary schools are from ethnic minority backgrounds (30% nationally).

Equally important is the fact that 17% of Catholic schools are in the most deprived areas of the country compared to 12% of other schools nationally.

How to use this book

This book is organised into two parts. In Part I we have focused on practical advice and suggestions as well as the opportunity to listen to parents, pupils and those already in work speaking about how they view Catholic education and what difference it may or may not have made to them. Part II looks at the mission of the Church in education in more depth and who is responsible for the school.

At the end of each chapter you will find five family discussion points and a reflection for you and your family to discuss and think about. This is important because parents/carers are the first educators of their children. The importance of the family is something that the Church returns to time and time again.

> *The family remains the basic unit of society and the first school in which children learn the human, spiritual and moral values which enable them to be a beacon of goodness, integrity and justice in our communities.*
>
> Pope Francis, Meeting with the Leaders of the Apostolate of the Laity, Korea, 16 August 2014

Chapter 1 offers guidance on what you should look for before selecting a school and then highlights how to go about the application process. This chapter also looks at some of the questions that parents ask about Catholic schools and whether or not their application will be considered.

Parents' views and expectations are expressed in Chapter 2 as we listen to a diverse range of parents talking about how they view Catholic education and what they hope for from a Catholic school.

Getting your child ready to start in a Catholic school is important. Children and young people settle far more quickly if they don't feel everything is new or strange. Chapter 3 seeks to offer you an overview of the basic things that your child needs to know, understand and be able to do before starting school – in particular, key prayers and ideas for you as a family to use and develop in your own way.

Listening to young people talking about their hopes and dreams as well as their experiences in a Catholic school in Chapter 4 provides first-hand evidence of the high expectations and formation for leadership. One cannot help but be impressed by the levels of social awareness of the younger pupils as well as their expectations of leaders today. Their letter to the Prime Minister makes interesting reading. It is interesting to listen to teenagers as they speak honestly about their years in Catholic schools and how much it has impacted on their lives.

Chapter 5 takes you into the world of work to see what difference having a Catholic education and formation might make. We ask people to say how well they feel a Catholic school prepares young people for work; does it make any difference?

In Chapter 6 you will find an overview of what the Church, governors and school hope for in the way of support from parents and carers. Don't be put off by the references to Canon Law in this chapter because it is important for you to have a clear understanding of what the Church actually expects. You will also find suggestions to help you become further involved.

In Part II of this book, Chapter 7 moves into the deeper level of understanding of the mission of the Church in education. This is particularly important because it outlines the reasons why the Church has long valued having its own schools. However, today there are many challenges and even threats facing all faith schools. As surprising as it may seem that any society would wish to get rid of its best schools, the humanist, secularist views do grab headlines and parents are often confused by their claims that Catholic schools are poor, divisive, selective and not serving those on the margins of society. The evidence from Ofsted demonstrates that this is clearly wrong and very unhelpful. However, governors will do their best to admit as many pupils as possible according to their admissions criteria and work in partnership with other schools to see that your child's needs are met. It is true that in oversubscribed areas there are many disappointed parents and children who will be unsuccessful in their applications.

Who holds the responsibility for Catholic schools and their performance is dealt with in Chapter 8 as it explains the role of the bishop, the diocese and governors.

Catholic schools hold a central role in the mission of the Church and as such are the major interface between the Church and younger generations of Catholics in this country. They do not replace the parish or the family's commitment to the practice of their faith, but are essential in keeping the links between the home, the school and the parish and the building up of community.

All education, if it is to be worthy of the title education, must be about the pursuit of truth:

Education cannot be neutral. It is either positive or negative; either it enriches or it impoverishes; either it enables a person to grow or it lessens, even corrupts… The mission of schools is to develop a sense of truth, of what is good and beautiful.

Pope Francis, Address to Students and Teachers from Schools across Italy, 10 May 2014

The Church seeks for her schools that they be places of learning where young people may find the true meaning of life in all its fullness through the beauty of learning as they seek to understand the mysteries of God through many different disciplines and experiences.

If something is true, it is good and beautiful; if it is beautiful; it is good and true; if it is good, it is true and it is beautiful. And together, these elements enable us to grow and help us to love life, even when we are not well, even in the midst of many problems. True education enables us to love life and opens us to the fullness of life.

Pope Francis, Address to Students and Teachers from Schools across Italy, 10 May 2014

PART I

CHAPTER 1

What should I look for and how do I get my child into a Catholic school?

The whole process of applying for a place in a school can be both stressful and confusing. Finding the right school is not easy. If this is your first child of school age, or you have just moved into a new area, it can appear rather daunting.

The following guidelines are offered to help you in the process.

STEP 1

Visit your parish priest and ask him about the local Catholic schools or go online and search for Catholic schools near you.

STEP 2

Go onto the school's website and look carefully at all aspects of the school. Make a note of anything you don't understand or want to know more about. Here is a brief outline of each of the key areas that you may need to know more about. For example:

The mission statement

> *Our family at St Joseph's learns, loves and grows with God at the centre.*
>
> St Joseph's Catholic Primary School, Islington, London

Inspire. Achieve. Serve.

John F. Kennedy Catholic School, Hemel Hempstead, Hertfordshire

The mission statement is an important starting point for the whole school because it serves to unite everyone as a learning community with the same common goals. Every school has its own unique statement, but they all express their particular way of fulfilling the mission of the Church in education.

Having drawn up a list of the schools you would like to visit, make a note of the things that you want to check out and the questions you would like to ask. Don't be nervous about doing this as the school is wanting to share as much information with you as possible. Look for evidence of the mission statement being lived out in practice. Does it really underpin everything the school does or is it just a sentence or two that is posted on the walls and never gets any further? The pupils always give you the really honest answers and you will be impressed – hopefully!

Governors and teachers

Find the website button labelled "governors". By opening this page you should find photos and information about each governor. Most schools also do the same with staff, letting you know who is teaching in what area and their position in the school. Contact details are not displayed as all communication must be through the school and not directly to the individual governor or member of staff.

If you are able to get to the school's open day or evening, seek out a governor and talk to her or him about the school and the governor's roles. Governors will be delighted that you recognise that they play a key role and will be very helpful. Many of them may well have children at the school.

Catholic life of the school

By looking at the website you will find information on Religious Education, the chaplaincy provision, the liturgical life of the school, prayer and worship, charity work and a whole range of activities and celebrations that form the distinctive nature of a Catholic school.

Academic standards and achievement

Religious Education is the core of the core curriculum in a Catholic school. It is the most important area of learning.

Religious Education is not one subject amongst many, but the foundation of the entire education process. The beliefs and values it communicates should inspire and unify every aspect of school life.

The Education Reform Bill: A Commentary for Catholics, Bishops' Conference of England and Wales, 1988

Catholic schools must provide 10% taught curriculum time to Religious Education in order to cover what is known as the *Bishops' Religious Education Curriculum Directory*. This is a document written by the bishops of England and Wales which lays out what must be taught at each key stage. It is then left to the professional expertise of the teachers to make this relevant and interesting for the pupils.

Spiritual, moral, social and cultural education

The first entitlement of the nation's children in all schools is to be spiritually, morally, socially and culturally educated (SMSC) (Education Reform Act 1988).

The table below will help you understand what each of these areas means.

Table: Defining SMSC education

Spiritual	Signifies what we believe about the meaning and purpose of life. Engaging in the big questions of purpose and meaning.
	It is everything about existence on this planet that is beyond the material. Our story.
Moral	Because of what we believe about the purpose and meaning of life we live by principles and codes which guide our choices between right and wrong.
Social	Our way of relating to self and others, which is influenced by our spirituality and our morality.
Cultural	The ways in which we do things – the rites, rituals, customs and practices that develop over time within communities. Culture gives expression to a community's spirituality, morality and social values.

What you are looking for is how links and connections are being made across all subjects. One way of doing this is by asking what are called "the big questions" of purpose and meaning of life. Each subject leader is responsible for identifying moments or interventions when these areas or questions may be raised and explored. In Chapter 3 you will hear Matyl talking about her science lesson and how she was suddenly asked about creation and evolution. What her science teacher was doing was making connections between the different areas of learning.

In doing so Matyl discovered that she needed both science and RE to inform each other. These links and bridges are open questions, which encourage the pupils to think more deeply and critically about life and the world they are living in.

All areas of your child's learning should be permeated through with Christian beliefs and values. You will notice that SMSC is inspected during Ofsted by both the Section 48 and Section 5 teams.

Pupil voice and involvement in the running of their school

Pupil voice is an important part of the school community. Governors, teaching and support staff are always seeking ways of ensuring that they really are meeting the needs of the children. You should discover things like:

- Pupil chaplaincy teams

- Liturgy teams

- Peer mentors/mediators

- School councils

- Caritas ambassadors

- Mini Vinnies (SVP)

- Pupil parliament

- Justice and peace groups

- Buddies

- Prefects

- Eco councils.

All of these pupil-led school initiatives and areas of responsibility are indicators that the school is not only listening to its pupils but also empowering them to step up and take responsibility.

Parent participation

Schools work hard to support parents with their child's learning and development. However, schools are communities and every individual person matters and is valued. Therefore parents are encouraged to work with the school for the common good of everyone. Regular newsletters go out in some schools weekly, half-termly or at least once a term. Have a look at the school website and you should discover a button labelled "newsletter". Some schools also have a texting system to parents' mobile phones for instant contact, especially when there is good news to share.

Schools have a variety of parent associations and areas where parents are encouraged to be involved. You will see information about this on the school's website but you should also find that the parents' association or friends of the school are present on open days and evenings to share with you all that they do and how new parents to the school can be involved.

Parents often find that primary schools are easier to access than a big secondary school. That's natural, simply because of the sheer size of many secondary schools. However, don't be put off. Once you get to know the school you should find it very welcoming.

Parental satisfaction with the school is very important. Many schools conduct surveys about various aspects of the school to keep abreast of how parents are feeling and ways in which the school might improve. You will also find that Ofsted has a "Parent View" questionnaire about the school, which feeds directly into Ofsted.

Understanding the Ofsted reports (Sections 48 and 5)

In a Catholic school the Ofsted report is in two parts. Section 48 is the section that deals with two main areas – classroom religious education and the Catholic life of the school. (Some dioceses, such as the Diocese of Salford, have a different model, but in the main they are covering the same areas as laid down by the bishops of England and Wales and Canon Law.) The inspection is carried out by two separate teams of inspectors. The Section 5 team is made up of Ofsted inspectors and the Section 48 by the bishop's inspection team. The bishop's team will focus on the following:

Classroom Religious Education

The focus here is on how religiously literate pupils are in the teachings and traditions of the Catholic faith and how well they know, understand and appreciate the importance of religious faith, which includes other faiths, and practice in everyday life. The term "religiously literate" means that your child is able to know and understand what they have been studying in RE and can use correct religious terminology and engage confidently in debate about the topic to an appropriate level.

To what extent is this achieved through:

* delivery of the Curriculum Directory;

* the quality of teaching;

* pupil achievement, attainment and progress;

* the effectiveness of the leadership and management of Religious Education?

The Catholic life of the school

How well does the school provide pupils with an integration of faith and life through a Catholic way of living and believing in all areas of school life? To what extent is this achieved through:

* the place of Religious Education as the core of the curriculum – time, staffing, accommodation, resources, budget;

* the experience of Catholic worship – prayer and liturgy – for the whole school community;

* the commitment and contribution to the common good – service and education in the social teaching of the Church – justice;

* the effectiveness of the leadership and management, including governors, in promoting the Catholic life of the school?

In schools with a religious character, section 5 inspectors must not comment on the content of religious worship or on denominational religious education (RE). Inspectors may visit lessons and assemblies in order to help them evaluate how those contribute to pupils' spiritual, moral, social and cultural development and their personal development, behaviour and welfare.

The governors and head teacher are always keen to have feedback from families about the teaching of RE and the Catholic life of the school, because they are the primary reason for the existence of the school. Some parents mistakenly think that the Section 5 inspection is more important than the Section 48, which is quite wrong.

The Section 5 Ofsted team will focus on:

Effectiveness of leadership and management

This is at every level in the school, starting with governance, which is now coming under very close scrutiny as to how effective it is in setting the strategic direction of the school and monitoring its effectiveness. The inspectors will evaluate the strength and effectiveness of the head teacher and the leadership of the team as a whole as well as middle leaders and the ways in which leadership is fostered across the school.

Quality of teaching, learning and assessment

This covers all areas of the curriculum. However, the Ofsted *School Inspection Handbook* (September 2015) states that:

Personal development, behaviour and welfare

The inspection of personal development came into the framework in 2015. Some parts of the content in this section on pupils' personal development have long been in the curriculum and life of the school. The challenge is how to evidence and assess it effectively.

Outcomes for pupils

This judgement is all about current standards and progress, including the school's own performance information. Based on evidence from data, observations of teaching, discussions with pupils and looking at their work, the inspectors will judge how well all pupils are progressing and being prepared for their next stage in learning or work.

What the school focuses on as being important

Academic learning is at the heart of the core purpose of a school. What is important to identify is what is driving the learning in the school. Of course the pupils must achieve the very best results possible, but if that is the end goal then the school as a Catholic learning community may not be fulfilling its mission.

Academic excellence is for a purpose. Catholic education strives to educate all children to be the very best they can be so that they can take their place in society, where necessary challenge what is not just or right, and have the insight and skill to know how to bring about change. In doing so they will play their part in the mission of the Church for the transformation of society.

How inclusive is it? Special Educational Needs and Disabilities (SEND)

Children with special educational needs and disabilities are a top priority within a Catholic school. Part of its mission is to have a preferential option for those in the greatest need. However, for parents with children who need specialised support, getting this help can often be very difficult. Every school has a specialist member of staff who has the responsibility of supporting children and their families who come into this category. You will find information on the website about this, and again don't hesitate to ask about the SEND provision on your visit.

Policies and procedures

These are many! They will be displayed on the website and they should be readily available to parents on request. All policy documents are regularly reviewed by the governors and where necessary adjusted in line with pupil needs and legal requirements.

STEP 3

Visit the school of your choice and speak to as many people as possible. You are looking to see if this is really right for your child's education and development. Other opinions are important, but your choice must be guided by the individual needs of your child. Don't be afraid to take your child with you. He or she will spot things that you don't. In the end it has to be your decision because you can see the bigger picture. Check the admissions criteria to see how your child may fare in the admissions process. You will see on the website and in the school brochure that the school has set admissions criteria. Once more, if you are not sure about the criteria, then ask at the school.

STEP 4

Filling in the correct application forms

It is essential that you fill in the correct application forms for the school. For a Catholic school there are two sets of forms and it is very important that you fill in both sets. If you are in doubt or not sure how to fill the forms in don't be afraid to ask at the school. The school website will give you clear directions on how to obtain both application forms.

Check the criteria for entry

Before you begin filling in the form, read through the criteria for oversubscription very carefully. If you know the school to be oversubscribed, then this will give you an indication of how strong your application is going to be. If the school is not oversubscribed with baptised Catholics, then if your child is a baptised Catholic you will have a strong case for a place.

Here is a typical example of an oversubscription set of criteria from a Catholic primary school (secondary schools are very similar):[1]

Where there are more applications for places than the sixty available, applicants will be placed in the following categories, listed in order of priority:

1. Catholic "looked-after" children and Catholic children who have been adopted or made subject to child arrangements orders or special guardianship orders immediately after having been looked after.

2. Baptised Catholic children from practising Catholic families living in (area is then defined).

3. Other baptised Catholic children from practising Catholic families living in neighbouring parishes without a Catholic school attached (area is then defined).

4. Baptised practising Catholic children.

5. Other baptised Catholic children.

6. Other Local Authority "looked-after" children and children who have been adopted or made subject to child arrangements orders or special guardianship orders, immediately after having been looked after.

7. Catechumens and Christians of other denominations whose parents wish them to have a Catholic education and whose application is supported by their minister of religion.

8. Any other applicants whose parents wish them to have a Catholic education and can provide written evidence from a religious leader of the regular practice of their faith.

9. Any other applicants where offering places to all applicants in any category would lead to oversubscription – priority will be given as follows:

   i. Exceptional circumstances: governors will give top priority within each criterion to applications where professional evidence, supplied at the time of application, indicates that the applicant has a compelling need to attend St… Catholic Primary School. Such evidence must be supplied by such as a doctor, social worker or priest.

   ii. Siblings of pupils who will be in attendance at the school at the start date of the new entrant. Siblings are defined as a brother or sister, adopted and half-brothers/sisters living at the same address, not including cousins or other extended family members who reside in the household, but will include stepbrothers/sisters and foster children who are part of the Catholic family.

   iii. The proximity of the address point for the home address to the centre point of the school measured by a straight line on the Ordnance Survey map, using (name of location) computerised mapping system, in cases where applicants live equal distance from the school and places cannot be offered to both children,

---

[1]   Reprinted with permission from St Bernadette's Catholic Primary School, Kenton, London.

a random allocation, i.e. lottery, will take place in the presence of an independent witness.

iv. Multiple births: governors will take the opportunity to admit twins/triplets siblings applying for the same academic year, where one child has been offered a place and the other(s) have not. This will most commonly be by admitting a second twin and going over the infant class size limit.

The Local Authority "Common Application Form"

In accordance with the Local Authority (LA) requirements, applicants must complete the LA "Common Application Form" (CAF) from their own LA. The CAF is obtainable from both the school office and the LA admissions service. The CAF allows you to nominate up to six schools in order of preference. You *must* submit only one CAF by the specified date of return. If you do not submit by the closing date your application will be at risk. If you submit more than one CAF, the last CAF received will replace an earlier submitted CAF.

School's own Supplementary Information Form (SIF)

Applicants should complete and return the school's own Supplementary Information Form (SIF). The SIF is obtainable from the school office or website. This is essential for a place in a Catholic school.

Priest's Reference Form

You must also obtain a Priest's Reference Form from the school or parish and hand it to the parish priest when completed. Many parishes have special dates for doing this so watch the newsletter for this information. In big parishes it is very difficult for the priest to put names to faces. It helps to take your child with you. The diocesan Priest's Reference Form is also available on your diocesan website. Parents/carers should provide the stipulated documentation including the child's proof of date of birth and baptismal certificates.

Returning the SIF

The SIF should be returned directly to the school office by the specified closing date. If any of the evidence in the SIF is found to be fraudulent or wrong in any way then the place may be withdrawn. Practising Catholics and those applying for categories 2, 3 and 4 of the criteria (see p.17) need to supply a Priest's Reference Form.

If you are applying to another Catholic school you will be required to complete a set of supplementary papers for each Catholic school.

Pupils with a Statement of Special Educational Needs/Education, Health and Care Plan (EHC)

The admission of pupils with a Statement of Special Educational Needs or Education Health and Care Plan (EHC) is dealt with by a completely separate procedure as set out in the Special Educational Needs Code of Practice – you can find this on the school's website. If your child has a Statement of SEN or EHC plan you must contact your local authority SEN officer. Children with Statements of SEN or EHC plans naming this school will be admitted.

Applicants must provide proof of their residential address. The two acceptable forms of documentation are either a current Council Tax letter or a current Child Benefit book/letter. Independent verification may be sought of the applicant's residential address.

If your application for a place at St... Catholic Primary School is refused you will have the right of appeal (*closing date...*) to the Independent Appeal Panel.

Unsuccessful applicants

These will be offered a place on a waiting list maintained for each year group. If a place becomes available this will be allocated in accordance with the school's admissions policy and oversubscription criteria. Places on the waiting list will be held open for a period until the end of Year 6 when the child would have left the school.

In-year admissions

Applications for in-year admissions are made directly to the school using a Common Application Form. If a place is available and there is no waiting list the child will be admitted. If there is a waiting list, then

applications will be ranked by the governing body in accordance with the oversubscription criteria. If a place cannot be offered at this time then you may ask them for the reasons and you will be informed of your right of appeal. You will be offered the opportunity of being placed on a waiting list. This waiting list will be maintained by the governing body in the order of the oversubscription criteria and not in the order in which the applications are received. When a place becomes available the governing body will re-rank the list so that an offer can be made.

Fair access protocols

The school is committed to taking its fair share of children who are vulnerable and/or hard to place, as set out in locally agreed protocols. Accordingly, outside the normal admissions round, the governing body is empowered to give absolute priority to a child where admission is requested under any local protocol that has been agreed by both the diocese and the governing body for the current school year. The governing body has this power even when admitting the child would mean exceeding the published admission number.

Admission of children outside their normal age group

Any application for a child to be educated out of his/her age group will be considered by governors on an individual basis and will only be granted in exceptional circumstances. Parents should write to the Chair of governors during the autumn term in the academic year of application, giving reasons and providing compelling professional evidence. If governors give permission for the child to be educated out of his/her normal age group, parents must submit an application in the normal way. This application will be treated in the same way as all other applications and there is no guarantee that an offer will be made.

Deferred entry

Applicants may defer entry to school up until statutory school age, i.e. the first day of term following the child's fifth birthday. Application is made in the usual way and then the deferral is requested. The place will then be held until the first day of the spring or summer term as applicable. Applicants may also request that their child attend part-time until statutory school age is reached. Entry may not be deferred beyond statutory school age or beyond the year of application, therefore applicants whose children have birthdays in the summer term may only defer until 1 April *of the following year.*

What is a Catholic academy?

An academy is essentially an independent school that is funded by the State. It is independent of the Local Authority and receives its funding direct from central government.

No Catholic school can become an academy without the consent of the bishop and the trustees of the diocese.

Admissions to Catholic academies

A voluntary aided Catholic school already deals with its own admission arrangements. As an academy, it would still deal with its own admission arrangements and would be bound by the national admissions code

and admissions appeals code. Therefore there will be no change in the way in which the admission arrangements are set for an academy.

As with all voluntary aided Catholic schools if an academy wanted to change its admission arrangements consultation would be required in the same way that it is for all state schools.

Frequently asked questions about admissions

I am a Catholic but I never got round to getting my child baptised. Will my child be admitted to a Catholic school?

This can be an issue if you are applying to an oversubscribed Catholic school. When parents ask for baptism at a later date this may be interpreted by some priests as showing that parents are not serious about practising their faith and are only seeking baptism as a way into a good school. Undoubtedly this does happen. On the other hand there are cases where for a variety of valid reasons the child has not been baptised. This is a moment to talk with your parish priest and explain your circumstances. Usually the parish priest will be only too happy to help you and enrol you in the baptismal preparation classes.

We are all baptised Catholics but it is not possible to go to Mass very often. Will this be ok?

This is another common scenario. What is important is to speak with your priest about this. In my experience I have encountered many parents who because of their work or difficulties with caring for someone at home do not always find it easy to get to Mass. However, there are many things that you can do with your children to keep their faith meaningful and vibrant. (See Chapter 3 for ideas.)

Our children have not been at a Catholic primary school, will this go against us?

At secondary level if your child is baptised then there should be no problem, particularly if you are coming from an area where there are not enough primary places.

We are Christians but not Catholic, but we really want our children to go to the Catholic school as there is no other Christian school near us. Will this be possible?

The admissions criteria will show you that there are places for children of other denominations if the school is not oversubscribed.

What about families who are from other faiths?

Once a school has accepted all the pupils who are baptised Catholics or who fall into the special category of cared-for children, then if there are vacancies the admissions criteria will be applied to each of those children who are not Catholic and those who have the highest rating according to the criteria will be offered the spare places.

Our child did not get a place – what next?

In a Catholic school the right to admit a child to the school lies with the governors of that school. Therefore you may appeal to the governors to reconsider your application. There is a set procedure for this process, which you will need to follow. Many schools will have a waiting list and you can ask to be put on that. An example of the procedure at one school is as follows:

If a place cannot be offered at this time then you may ask us for the reasons and you will be informed of your right of appeal. You will be offered the opportunity of being placed on a waiting list. This waiting list will be maintained by the governing body in the order of the oversubscription criteria and not in the order in which the applications are received. When a place becomes available the governing body will re-rank the list so that an offer can be made.

The school will give you all the advice you need about how to appeal.

POINTS FOR FAMILY DISCUSSION

- Are there any questions related to this chapter that you are still wondering about? Talk together about these and if necessary contact your parish priest/ pastoral assistant to help you.
- Have a look at some Ofsted reports (Section 48 and 5) for schools you might be interested in. Discuss these findings together.
- What impression do you get from local Catholic school websites about the centrality of Religious Education, its importance and the importance of the Catholic life of the school?

- If practical ask the parents of children who go to a school you are interested in if you can meet with them as a family to talk about their experiences of the school.
- If your child is not successful in getting a place in a Catholic school, how will you continue to bring her or him up in the faith?

Reflection based on Romans 8:14-17

Lord and creator of all people,
with Jesus your Son we say,
"Abba, Father".
Your Holy Spirit joins with our
spirit, showing us that we are
your children.
Guide our hearts and minds that
each member of our family may
strive to be the people you have
created us to be.
Amen.

CHAPTER 2

Parent views

Researching the right school

Finding the right school for your child can be a real challenge. That is why it is so important to go to visit as many schools as you can. All schools have a web page where you can find a great deal of information. Have a look at their mission statement, aims and values as well as how much attention is given to the Catholic life of the school, prayer formation, spiritual, moral, social and cultural education and of course the teaching of Religious Education. You will also be able to download their latest diocesan Ofsted report (Section 48) and the Ofsted Section 5 report. These documents will give you a great deal of information.

However, they are not the full picture and schools can change very quickly. So it is important to see for yourself and draw your own conclusions.

Having drawn up your shortlist of possible schools, look for information about their open days/nights and visit the school yourself. If possible ask to visit the school during the working day to see it in action. This can be difficult for working parents. However, schools are usually only too happy to make arrangements to accommodate you. Ask all the questions you want to. Don't be shy because it is the head teacher. He or she will be only too happy to discuss any issues you may have. If possible talk to the children. They are the ones who really know what life is like in the school.

The Gowda family

Rakesh and Julia, why did you choose a Catholic school?

Rakesh: I was educated in a Catholic school although I am from a Hindu family. We both wanted to find a school where our son Janek would experience the same values that are important to us. Having had so much experience of Catholic education, I was very happy when we got a place at St Anselm's.

Julia: We both want our children to be educated in a holistic way. We want Janek to grow up knowing who he is, make the right choices and to be a well-rounded good person.

Rakesh: For me respect for other people, their cultures and way of life is very important. We are a multi-faith, multicultural family and it is important for our son to know who he is and what he believes. I see him developing well at St Anselm's.

Julia: Yes, St Anselm's is a very multicultural school but it has a clear Catholic identity and really reflects the diversity of the Catholic Church. We are delighted that Janek is being educated in a context which will help him make the right choices as an adult.

How does the school support you in educating Janek?

Julia: We have a lot of information about his progress but one thing we really appreciate is the "Wednesday Word" which Janek makes sure we all discuss and think about the Sunday Gospel passage. It's a great way of talking about our faith and sharing our thoughts.

Janek: I really like my school. It is fun. One of the best things was our First Holy Communion. We all made it together which was really good.

The Ampoma family

Cynthia, what made you chose a Catholic school for Sherna?

Cynthia: I grew up and was educated in Ghana and when I came to this country I wanted my children to have the same education and formation as I had. There is so much talk today about getting rid of Catholic schools but I totally disagree. Parents must have the choice to bring their children up and have them educated as they wish. The government wants us all to be the same, herded in one direction. That is not what parents want. My daughter is being educated within our beliefs and values as Christians. She is learning to pray in many different ways and everything the school does is guided by the mission statement, "We aim for excellence in all we think, do and say, using the gifts God has given us, using our spiritual, academic, and physical potential. LOVE, RESPECT, HONESTY and UNDERSTANDING." This is what I want for my daughter.

Do you think the school is preparing Sherna for life today?

Cynthia: Absolutely! What I like is they teach to a very high standard but also make all the links and connections with other subjects and everyday life. The children understand why they are learning. It all makes more sense. My daughter is given responsibility and a lot is expected of her. We like that.

Sherna, how do you feel about being in a Catholic school?

Sherna: I really love my school. Our head teacher is very funny. I wish he had his own class and I could be in it! All our teachers are kind to the children and they really show us how to learn more about God and this makes me want to learn more. One thing I want to be when I am in Year 5 is a pupil chaplain like my brother Jerome. He gets to do some lessons in the younger classes, and lead prayers and even do Bible story telling in assembly in front of the whole school. But I am only in Year 3 so I will have to wait. I hope I get picked.

What do you find exciting in your school, Sherna?

Sherna: Lots of things. This year I get to make my First Communion and I am really excited about that. I also like my lessons and I want to do really well then I can be a doctor when I am older.

Cynthia, how does the school strengthen your links with the parish?

Cynthia: The sacramental preparation programme is really good. Parents get a lot of help through classes to develop their faith as well as support the teaching that the children get in school. Our parish priest comes into school very often and we love to see him and he knows us all. It is important to have the school and the parish supporting families.

The O'Sullivan family

Monica, why did you select a faith school?

Monica: Life is very different today compared to when I was growing up. Children need a very clear moral compass to guide them through often difficult and complex decisions even at a young age. What amuses us as parents is the way in which our children actually keep us in line! My husband and I are quickly corrected if we say or do anything we shouldn't.

How do you see the home and the school working in partnership?

Monica: In this school it is very strong. Nothing gets missed and the children know that. I can come in at any time and someone will help with whatever the issue is. The same is true if there is something the school wants to communicate, especially if it is good news.

How independent do you think the school helps your child to be?

Monica: We have seen this developing in all our children. The school does not tell them what to do or think but rather challenges and empowers them to know how to make good choices. We don't always get it right, but they do know the difference between right and wrong and why that is the case. For our family it is important that the same social and moral standards are accepted at home, in school and in the parish community, so that the children experience a joined-up life.

The Reidy family

Maggie, what guided your choice of a Catholic education for Eva?

Maggie: More than anything we wanted Eva to learn and grow in a Catholic school community, which reflects who we are and what is important to our family. We have three children, two are in the school at the moment. Life is so complex today that it is not easy for young people. My husband and I went to Catholic schools and it gave us a solid foundation on which to base our lives. We want the same for all our children. All the Catholic schools in our borough are very good or outstanding. In our school the academic standards are very high. But that is not the only area that is impressive. As well as the National Curriculum, Catholic schools teach values and provide a fundamental foundation for a young person to grow and develop within the Catholic faith.

Wouldn't all schools say that?

Maggie: Yes and no! We really did our homework in trying to find the right school. It is important to visit different schools and make sure you talk to the head teacher as well as the staff and if possible some of the children. Ofsted reports are helpful, but they are not the full picture and they may be out of date. We found something unique in this school. The children are taught who they are as God's children; we are family here and all have a common story as a faith community. You don't get that in non-faith schools.

The Jackson family

Peter and Sandra, what attracted you to a Catholic secondary school for your children?

Peter: I am not a Catholic but when we got married I undertook to support Sandra in bringing our children up in the Catholic faith. I feel very positive about it. Yes, it was an obligation I committed to. However, having also been the parent governor of my children's primary school for six years, I came to really appreciate the way in which the beliefs and values ran through every aspect of the school's learning and life.

Sandra: As a child I began my schooling in a non-Catholic school and then at secondary level moved to a Catholic school, so I have experienced both. I preferred the Catholic school experience because it was more rounded. I felt secure in exploring my ideas and beliefs in a safe environment. This is really important particularly for teenagers. I want Orla and Jude to feel the same and be able to be themselves.

Orla and Jude, how do you feel about being in a Catholic secondary school?

Orla: I really like the community. I moved on with my friends from primary school and that made a big difference. We went as friends from primary school, though we have met many new friends too. Now we are all preparing for confirmation and that is really great because we are in it together. We can share our experiences, thoughts and events like retreats. I sometimes serve at Mass in school as well as in the parish. We have a lot of help in learning about our faith. We don't just learn about the Catholic faith but other faiths as well. It is very interesting. I like being part of a family and that is what we are.

Jude: I have just started in my secondary school. I love it because most people are really friendly. The pastoral care always tries to meet our needs and there are an awful lot of us! I like being able to go the voluntary Mass and we sometimes have reconciliation. You can just go and no one makes fun of you or thinks it is odd. I feel safe and can be myself, it helps me to feel closer to God.

Do you feel that the children are being sufficiently challenged academically?

Peter: Academic excellence is the core purpose of a school. So yes, for me it is of primary importance. Both our children are challenged and doing well and we are kept informed of their progress. I have noticed that Jude has really bought into the culture of his new school and accepted the increased challenges and is positive about learning.

Sandra: Academic learning is naturally key, but it needs to be conducted in a holistic or rounded way. We looked for schools that would treat our children as individuals, find what they are good at and build on their gifts.

Why did you choose single-sex schools for your children?

Peter: We talked about this with both our children and in our area we are lucky because there is a wide choice of Catholic schools, more so than outside the Catholic sector. We visited several schools and these were the ones that we all agreed met the needs of each of our children as individuals. It was a family decision.

What has impressed you most about your children's schools?

Sandra: Beside the teaching and learning it has to be the very strong moral messages that permeate the schools. The Christian values of love, respect, forgiveness, inclusiveness and justice, to mention just a few, are everywhere. This was true of the primary schools as well. So both our children have moved into very different schools but the culture is the same.

Peter: For me it is the rhythm and framework of their school life. The liturgical calendar plays a big part in creating this natural rhythm. I agree with Sandra and the children in saying the cohesiveness of life is important. Home, school and parish community need to be in step.

The Kassouf family

How do you find Catholic schools in England compared with your home in Lebanon?

Gladys: I was afraid that it would be very different and my children would not have a strong Catholic environment to be educated in. At first we could not get all our children into a Catholic school, which was a real worry for us. But eventually we got places as people moved out of the parish. However, once all three of my girls were given a place we were really surprised at how committed people were and they clearly wanted the same as we did. Of course there are a few people who will say anything to gain a place in a Catholic school who never practise once their child gets in, but the majority are not like that in our school.

What about secondary education for Matyl?

Fady: We were unsure of what to do. So many choices, but it had to be the school that would really help Matyl to develop as a young woman in this country. We are not in Lebanon now and she needs to understand how to flourish here. We visited several schools and they all had particular strengths. I wanted a school that was not only academically outstanding but that would provide Matyl with a strong moral and spiritual direction. I think this is a feature of Catholic schools worldwide. When we lived in Lebanon it was interesting to see how many non-Christian parents would do anything to get their children into a Catholic school. This seemed strange to me because there were plenty of Muslim schools.

What I discovered from my Muslim friends was that they wanted a Catholic school for many reasons. Discipline was always high on their agenda as were academic standards but so was something much more important in today's world. They wanted their children to learn that forgiveness was stronger than vengeance. Catholic schools are recognised as being places where reconciliation is possible and in fact I have found that in many schools it is a key value which is reinforced through school policies and liturgies.

Matyl: When we visited Sacred Heart I was nervous. It was so big compared to my primary schools. But I like the atmosphere and there were girls from all over the world so I did not feel strange. Until now I have been in mixed schools, so going to an all-girls' school is something different. I like it. For me the biggest difference is in the amount of religious education. We have RE lessons but in our other subjects the teachers often bring up moral or religious questions. Sometimes I feel really confused. One day my science teacher asked us about evolution and what we thought. I did not know what to say and I was scared to say anything because I thought Catholics did not believe in evolution. So I asked my mum and she asked my cousin who is a medical scientist. She explained to me how theology and science go together, one shines a light of understanding on the other. She explained how religion is the inspiration and science is the application. I am going to say that in our next discussion. I like the way our teachers ask us really difficult questions. It makes you think even if it does leave you feeling a bit out of your depth.

Fady: You know there is a saying in scripture, "By their fruits you will know them." This is what I want said of my children. I see in Catholic schools here a real attempt to form young people to be who they are as Christians and how to act and behave and not follow the latest trend or stupid behaviour. All children are blessed by God. It is like the story of the five loaves and the two fish. Without God's blessing they remain just fish and bread. Once you recognise the blessing they become much more.

How well do you think your children's schools are preparing them for adult life?

Gladys: Family life and society are both very different here. Our culture is very family orientated and community based. Here you have to make much more of an effort to get to know people and become accepted as part of the community. However, I notice how confident the girls are becoming. Though they are sometimes shocked at what they see in society and even in school! They don't understand why people behave that way. But they are learning to deal with these things without feeling they have to adopt values that we consider to be wrong. The schools are really good at helping them to recognise that this country is very diverse and full of many people from all over the world with different cultures and religions and none. That is a real strength of being in a Catholic school because we have a common culture, beliefs and values. We belong to a global Church so it will be both familiar and strange.

Fady: While I want to protect my girls I am quite relaxed about the way in which they are being educated. They must learn to engage with different points of view and ideas. I think schools are very good at that here and it prepares them well for life after secondary school whatever they do.

How comfortable are you about expressing your faith today in this country?

Gladys: I know some people don't like to talk about religion or their faith. This is strange for us. I am not afraid to discuss my faith, but my problem is I don't know enough. I want to know more about my faith. This is not easy because I need someone to help me to understand.

Fady: The world is very different today from when we were at school. We accepted what we were taught and rarely questioned it. Today everything is questioned. I think our girls will find it easier than we do because their schools don't teach them so much what to think, they teach them how to think. That is what will carry them through many challenges as adults.

Matyl: I feel safe being a Catholic in Sacred Heart. We have a chapel and I go there sometimes just to be quiet. I am an altar server in my parish so I volunteer at Masses and sometimes I like to go to the weekly voluntary Mass. My friends do too. It is normal for us to talk about religion and problems today. There are a few pupils who think it is cool to be anti-religion and they will try to make you feel stupid for saying it is important to you, but we just say, "What's your problem?"

A unique outstanding learning community – Pield Heath House School

Sister Julie, as the Executive Principal of a school for children and young people with special educational needs, how can you help parents to educate their children?

Sister Julie: Our parents have to fight for absolutely everything. Life is an uphill struggle all the way. When they come to us we want them to know that nothing is insurmountable. Here at Pield Heath we will do all we can to help them get the very best for their children because that is what they deserve. We provide a holistic approach to education, within a caring, spiritual environment where every young person is of equal importance, valued for what they are and encouraged to reach their maximum potential. Our purpose is to maximise our students' life experience to enable their independence and inclusion in the wider community.

Sara and Dominic Moir share their thoughts about the difference being in a Catholic school has made to their daughter Charlotte and to them personally.

How do you feel the school is helping your child?

Sara: Charlotte has a severe learning difficulty. In her old primary school she was pulled out of class and taught in a separate room on a one-to-one basis. She is now learning to share space and resources with her peers. Although this wasn't easy at first she is now a much happier, more rounded child. Staff are accepting of Charlotte and work with her, challenging her in a gentle, holistic way. Charlotte is learning valuable life skills alongside the curriculum. The two are intertwined at Pield Heath. The school links the topics to everyday life. Staff make it clear what they expect from her and she is learning that good behaviour is the better, more rewarding option. They bring out Charlotte's positive side and deal with anything negative with patience and understanding. She is a happier, better-behaved child.

What difference does it make being in a Catholic school?

Dominic: I believe the school provides a great moral compass and provides spiritual direction for Charlotte. The Christian values throughout the school teach Charlotte about friendship, forgiveness, hope and endurance. I feel she is part of a family at Pield Heath. The faith foundation of the school provides an extension of the Catholic family ethos in which Charlotte and her two sisters are brought up, an ethos supported and encouraged by both sets of grandparents. In addition, we are keen for Charlotte to receive the sacrament of confirmation. The fact that she can do this under the care of Pield Heath is a great comfort to us.

As parents, how do you feel supported by the school?

Sara: I've never felt so supported since joining Pield Heath. When Charlotte was struggling with her behaviour the school couldn't have done more. I trusted them completely and they didn't let me down. A team of people were there for us; I was welcomed to the school to talk through strategies and kept fully informed via various mediums. As a result I have a very different, much happier child. I receive a daily written account and weekly photographic evidence. If anything happens, such as a fallout between her and a friend, Charlotte's class teacher will telephone to talk through the incident with me so I can fully understand and support Charlotte.

What aspects of the school do you really like?

Sara: I like everything about the school. I love that the children have Mass once a week, I love that the school canteen feels so calm and feels more like a bistro than a canteen! I love how welcoming and calm the school is, how the children are rewarded for their efforts and good behaviour. Pield Heath is the best thing that has happened to Charlotte and I thank God for it every day.

Similar themes

Looking at these interviews, it is interesting to see that the same themes occur across all age groups. The sense of community, a holistic approach, inclusion, the importance of Religious Education, a strong awareness of right and wrong with a formation and confidence in tackling injustice. The diversity of cultures and religious backgrounds is also striking, particularly the fact that those interviewed saw this as an important strength of their education.

What about independent Catholic schools?

Mr Stephen Oliver is head teacher of Our Lady's, Abingdon, Oxford, an independent Catholic day school.

How would you advise undecided parents about the benefits of a Catholic education in an independent school?

Parents considering an education for their children in the Catholic independent sector can sometimes be unsure what we really mean when we say that our schools are "Catholic". "What difference does this actually make on a day-to-day basis?" is the question most likely to be posed. When there is a highly attractive non-Catholic alternative just down the road, why, when it comes to it, go for the Catholic option? In my experience this is not just something that non-Catholic parents want to explore – even our fellow Catholics need to be persuaded that a Catholic school is the right choice for their child.

The answer at one level is very simple: most Catholic independent schools are highly successful at what they do. They are schools that achieve excellent academic outcomes, offer a broad range of extra-curricular activities and provide outstanding pastoral care. But there is something much more fundamental too. Years working in our sector and meeting heads of similar schools have convinced me that there is a special quality about Catholic independent schools that, if you could bottle it, other schools would be desperate to have. It is what inspires our mission, directs our work of teaching and learning and offers, no less, a vision for the goal of human life.

What exactly is this quality?

In short, the fact that the education we provide is explicitly grounded in the person of Jesus Christ. Our whole approach springs from this source. A Christ-centred education is necessarily child-centred, in that it encourages us to see Christ in every child. This puts us at the forefront of the Church's mission as we reach out to those in our care and value them as children of God. We nurture pupils so that they receive a rounded education, achieving of their very best academically while at the same time growing as human beings. A lot of independent schools claim to do this – reading school websites can be boringly repetitive – but, in my experience, Catholic schools really do.

How would you sum up the specific contribution your school makes to the formation and education of the pupils at Our Lady's?

I cannot think of a better way of summing up what Catholic independent schools do than by quoting a few lines from an address Pope Francis gave to schoolchildren in 2013. As ever, Francis showed his ability to sum up in a few words what many people have struggled to express in whole volumes. He told the children:

School broadens not only your intellectual dimension, but also the human one. I would like to focus on two fundamental values: freedom and service. Before all else be free persons! Freedom means knowing how to reflect on what we do, knowing how to evaluate which are the behaviours that make us grow. It means always choosing the good. Being free to always choose the good is challenging, but it will make you persons with a backbone, who know how to face life. The second word is service. In your schools you participate in various activities that prepare you not to be wrapped up in yourselves or in your own little world, but to open yourselves to others, especially to the poorest and most in need, to work to improve the world we live in.

Freedom, the good, intellect, service: these words encapsulate the essence of the education we offer. Our mission, as Francis says, is to set children free to be themselves, to release their potential and become the people their gifts and talents show that they can be. Cultivation of the mind goes hand in hand with developing the whole person, giving our pupils a moral sense in an increasingly value-free world. Education cannot take place in a vacuum. That is why we encourage our students to engage with the world around them and contribute to the common good, both now and when they leave school. As well as ensuring they are given the knowledge they need to advance in their careers, we develop them as leaders, willing to approach the wider world with a sense of social responsibility.

These values are fundamental to our mission as Catholic schools and we invite every young person – whether Catholic or not – to share them. Intellectually curious young people, challenged to explore what makes life worth living, are far more likely to become balanced, well-rounded adults than those drilled in a more narrow school. It is this vision that makes our schools unique.

A variety of reasons

You will notice from all these families and teachers that the reasons why parents choose a Catholic school are very varied. What is important is that families and schools must work together in order to enable a holistic and rounded education and formation. High-level learning, discipline, respect, moral code – and in some cases it is reconnecting with their faith and culture. For others it is a safe environment, physically, morally and spiritually. Very often families cannot say why they want a Catholic school, but they feel welcome and at home. It is particularly important to reassure those parents who may have found it difficult to attend Mass regularly that the school is there not to replace their responsibilities but to support them in the religious formation of their children. Teachers are open to helping adults deepen their own faith through their children's learning and understanding. Schools are not there to judge parents but to journey with them.

POINTS FOR FAMILY DISCUSSION

- Share with your child your memories of being at school. What did you enjoy and what did you find difficult?
- What are the values you want your child to have and to be able to live out in daily life? Talk about these as a family.
- In the light of the testimonies in this chapter from different families, can you now identify more clearly why you wish your child to go to a Catholic school? Talk with your family members about this.
- Talk with your child about the uniqueness of a Catholic education and why it is important to you.
- Reflect together how you and your family are engaged in the life of your parish. Is there more you can do?

 Reflection based on Ephesians 1:16-19a

Spend a few moments reflecting on the words of St Paul in these verses being addressed to:

- You

- Your family.

CHAPTER 3
Pupils getting ready – what your child needs to know

Preparing your children for their new school should be an exciting time full of hope and expectation for all the family. The ease and speed with which they settle can be helped by good preparation beforehand. Today schools work hard to help pupils feel at home quickly. Pupils go through up to five times of transition in their academic life:

- Nursery/Reception (Foundation Stage)

- Infants (Key Stage 1) to Juniors

- Juniors (Key Stage 2) to Secondary

- Secondary (Key Stages 3-4) to Sixth Form

- Sixth Form (Key Stage 5) to College/University.

Getting ready to go school for the first time

In the months before your child starts school a member of staff will have visited you at home. Special familiarisation days and visits to the nursery or reception class all help to ease anxieties and nerves as the children become accustomed to their new surroundings. Your child will be excited about wearing his or her new uniform clothes and a school bag with all that he or she needs inside.

You can also help to prepare your child by making sure she or he is aware of some of the practices and prayers that you have already started at home. For parents who are not Catholic the following ideas may be useful to help you prepare for school.

Prayer

Prayer is very important in the life of a Catholic school. Children will experience the class praying together from their first day. This usually takes the form of the children gathering together on the carpet near their prayer table.

Try to find a time every day when you can have a quiet moment with your child to talk to Jesus and pray for special things that are important to the family as well as thanking God for all the blessings and good things of the day. You may find the best time for this is when the child is going to bed.

Setting up your family prayer corner

Identify a special focal point in your house for a prayer area. This may be in the child's bedroom or in a communal room. A simple table or shelf will be fine. Place in the prayer area religious pictures, or a statue, cross, Bible, candle or anything that is of religious significance to the family. This can serve as the prayer focal point for times of prayer for all the family.

The sign of the cross

Teaching your child to make the sign of the cross is a prayer in itself. Explain that this sign is really important. As we make it and say the words we are telling God that all that we are and everything we are doing is going to be for God. Practise it together slowly and with reverence. At each step think about the words and what they mean.

Examples

Using your right hand, touch your forehead and say,

"In the name of the Father"… pause…

then move your hand to touch the lower middle of your chest and say, "and of the Son"… pause…

then move your hand to the left shoulder as you say, "and of the Holy"…

and to the right shoulder as you say the word, "Spirit"… pause…

then bring your hands together and say, "Amen".

By slowing down the making of the sign of the cross you are introducing the child to the fact that this is a prayer.

Once your child has mastered the words and actions you can further develop this prayer by making a longer pause and add in further thoughts for each of the persons of the Blessed Trinity.

For example:

In the name of the Father… Thank you, Father, for making me and all my family. Help me to learn more and more about you every day.

…and of the Son… Jesus, I love you. Thank you for showing me how to love (names).

…and of the Holy Spirit… Thank you, Holy Spirit, for all the gifts you have given me (they can name them if they wish and ask the Holy Spirit to guide them).

For very young children the following prayers are difficult to understand. At this stage learning them by heart is very important. Gradually you can begin to explain where the prayer came from and what it actually means.

Praying the Hail Mary

The Hail Mary is taken from the words of the angel Gabriel's visit to Mary at the annunciation (Luke 1:28) and the visitation of Mary to Elizabeth.

Introduce the background to this prayer by telling the story of Mary's visit to Elizabeth when she found she was going to be the mother of Jesus. Talk about the time when you were waiting for your child to be born and all the things that you and the family did to get ready.

In those days Mary set out and went with haste to a Judean town in the hill country, where she entered the house of Zechariah and greeted Elizabeth. When Elizabeth heard Mary's greeting, the child leapt in her womb. And

*Elizabeth was filled with the Holy Spirit and
exclaimed with a loud cry, "Blessed are you
among women, and blessed is the fruit of your
womb. And why has this happened to me, that
the mother of my Lord comes to me? For as soon
as I heard the sound of your greeting, the child in
my womb leapt for joy. And blessed is she who
believed that there would be a a fulfilment of
what was spoken to her by the Lord."*

Luke 1:39-45

Hail Mary

Hail Mary, full of grace,
the Lord is with thee.
Blessed art thou among women
and blessed is the fruit of thy womb, Jesus.
Holy Mary, Mother of God,
pray for us sinners,
now and at the hour of our death.
Amen.

The Our Father or Lord's Prayer

You will find this version in the Gospel of Matthew
6:9-13, where Jesus is teaching the people how to pray:

*Pray then in this way:
Our Father in heaven,
hallowed be your name.
Your kingdom come.
Your will be done,
on earth as it is in heaven.
Give us this day our daily bread.
And forgive us our debts,
as we also have forgiven our debtors.
And do not bring us to the time of trial,
but rescue us from the evil one.*

Helping young children understand the Our Father

The Our Father is a prayer taken straight from
scripture and one that all Christians say. The words
are difficult for young children to understand, but it is
helpful if you give them some background to the
prayer. For example:

*One day some of Jesus' friends asked him how to
pray. This is what he taught them to say.
Jesus wanted us all to know that God is our Father.*

*God made everyone and loves us very much.
That is why we can call him "Our Father".
He wants us to always remember that we are his
family so we must look after one another as our
brothers and sisters. This is how people love each
other in heaven and we must try to do the same
every day.*

*We can ask our Father to look after us and have
the strength not to be unkind to anyone.
If we do sometimes fail we can ask our Father to
forgive us and we can try to forgive other people
who are not kind to us.*

*When we say the Our Father we are asking to
be very strong and not make the wrong choice.*

Making a family prayer book

Young children love to look at books, and nothing is better than books that they have made with you. In preparation for starting school choose a beautiful notebook, preferably with a hard cover, which will be suitable for sticking things in as well as writing and drawing. Explain that this is going to be their own prayer book to keep all the time that they are in their primary school.

Begin by explaining that they can draw, write when they are able to (till then you can scribe for them) and stick in special things they want to say to Jesus as well as listening to what he might be saying to them. For example, they could put in holy pictures, pictures of people they love and want to pray for, children's prayers that they like such as morning and night prayers.

Children's morning prayer

Dear Jesus, thank you for today.
May all I do and say
be my very best, come what may
in all my learning and in my play.
Amen.

Children's bedtime prayer

Dear Jesus, I love you very much.
Thank you for all my friends and family.
Thank you for all the good things today.
Look after us all tonight especially (names).
Amen.

Child's prayer for protection

Angel of God, my guardian dear,
to whom God's love commits me here;
ever this day, be at my side
to light and guard,
to rule and guide.

Examination of the day: giving thanks

Adult: Thank you, Jesus, for... *(people adult wants to name)*.

Child: Thank you, Jesus, for... *(people child wants to name)*.

Adult: Thank you, Jesus, for... *(event or something adult has seen)*.

Child: Thank you, Jesus, for... *(event or something child has seen)*.

Adult: Jesus, tonight please look after... *(name)*.

Child: Jesus, tonight please look after... *(name)*.

Adult: Jesus, I want to be the best I can. I am sorry that I... *(mention anything that could have been better or if forgot to remember to pray/think of Jesus and thank him during the day)*.

Child: Jesus, I want to be the best I can. I am sorry that I... *(mention anything that could have been better or if forgot to remember to pray/think of Jesus and thank him during the day)*.

Telling our faith story through the sacraments and important moments in the life of the family

Talk to your child about the very exciting times in their life so far. Look together at the first images that you have of your child: newly born or the very first pictures you have of them. Talk about how you and their family felt when they first saw them.

Baptism

Recall the day of your child's baptism. Look at photos and identify each of the family members and any gifts/cards they gave as a memento of the day.

Look again at the child's baptismal candle and talk about the picture on the candle.

Identify the godparents and say why you chose them. Say why the Church wants them to have godparents.

For example:

- To support the children in their knowledge and understanding of the faith.

- To help the parents in all their responsibilities in caring for and bringing up the children.

Talk together about the priest who baptised them. What did he do?

For example:

The priest welcomed you.

The priest and godparents made the sign of the cross on your forehead to show you belong to Jesus Christ.

Everyone prayed, asking all the saints in heaven to pray for you too.

We prayed that you will be strong and free from any sin.

The priest then anointed you with a special oil.

The priest then baptised you with water, saying, "(Name), I baptise you in the name of the Father, and of the Son, and of the Holy Spirit."

The priest anointed you again, this time with the oil of Chrism on your forehead to remind everyone that you are sharing with Jesus Christ in his role as a priest, prophet and king. (In Greek, the word "Christos" means "anointed.")

If possible show the child the special white garment that he or she was clothed in. Explain that this was used to show that the child is very close to Jesus in all he or she does – as close as the clothes we wear. This can be further explained by saying that we wear special clothes for doing different things. We put on our best clothes for very important occasions. Once we are baptised then we are trying to be as much like Jesus as we can all the time.

Look again at the baptismal candle: this candle is lit from the Paschal (Easter) candle and symbolises that your child now possesses the light of Christ in his or her heart. A baby cannot carry this candle, so the light is entrusted to the parents and godparents.

Explain how the priest then said important prayers over the child's ears and mouth so that they will be able to be opened to hearing the Good News of Jesus and proclaiming it to others.

Blessing of the parents: the rite of baptism ends with a prayer of blessing for the parents.

First reconciliation

In Year 3 of their primary school your child will begin preparation for the sacrament of reconciliation. (There are variations in some dioceses and this may be deferred to a later date.)

Children mature at different stages and their awareness of the difference between right and wrong also varies. Generally speaking, children do have some knowledge of when they are making the right choice and when they are not. Right from the start of the children's time at school, teachers and their assistants will be helping them to develop an understanding of right and wrong not only in their RE lessons but throughout all their learning.

First Communion

This is a very important moment for children. In many parishes First Holy Communion is usually in Year 3. However, both parishes and dioceses vary in practice for a variety of reasons. It is also true that because of families relocating from one part of the country to another or even from one country to another, parishes will find children being presented for First Holy Communion at an older age. The

general norm in England and Wales is for preparation to be carried out in the parish by catechists. However, there are still some places where this is not the case and preparation is through the Catholic school. Where the parish relies on the school to prepare children for the sacraments they also make provision for children who are not able to attend a Catholic school by providing special classes for them led by catechists.

Parishes also vary in how long this preparation lasts. In some cases it will be for several months with the parents being asked to attend classes separately from the children so that they can support them at home. This reflects the Church's belief that it is the parents who are the first educators in the faith of their children. So the parish prepares you, the parent, to teach your children. The model that is most common is that the children attend regular classes with the catechists each week and the parents attend a separate class perhaps once a month.

Clearly parishes vary according to needs. Therefore it is important to check with your parish priest well in advance. Both the school and the parish priest will inform you of dates for enrolment in First Communion classes and you should receive a full diary of dates. Although classes will be led by trained catechists, your participation is very important and attendance at the parent sessions is essential in order to support your child's learning and development.

It is not uncommon for some parents to feel somewhat at sea simply because they may have had very little religious education or instruction themselves. The main thing to remember is not to worry. Your parish catechists and teachers are there to support you. If in doubt ask for help. You won't be the only person feeling rather vulnerable!

The following are some simple but effective ways in which you can support the faith development of your child.

Seeing God present in our lives

Through people

Families are made up of a wide range of interesting and diverse people. Grandparents, aunts and uncles, and godparents may well be a resource you can draw on.

Begin with godparents or if they are not available try another relative. Invite them for a meal or to come and talk with their godchild. Share together how they feel about being a godparent, why they think being a person of faith is important, how they pray, special moments when they felt God was present to them. Talk about funny things that may have happened which showed that God has a great sense of humour.

In this special time of preparation maybe godparents might take their godchild for an outing to somewhere important and explain why they like this place.

Through pictures

Pictures are a wonderful means of recalling important moments, for example your baptism, First Communion, confirmation and any other key moments. Children and young people love to see and hear about life when the adult members of their family were young, even if it is rather embarrassing and you will come in for some serious teasing about your fashion sense! All you need to do is tell the story behind the pictures and let the questions from the child flow.

Through artefacts

All families have special items that have great sentimental or religious significance. Simply share these together, telling the story behind them. It might be a family rosary, religious picture, family Bible or statue that has been handed down from one generation to another. You will be pleasantly surprised at how interesting this can be and it is all part of the family's faith story.

Through places

Every family has somewhere that has a particular significance for them, which is connected with important times in their lives. In this fast-moving society that our young people are growing up in many have little or no idea of the journey that their family has been on. Organise a family pilgrimage to "meet the ancestors", revisiting some places of significance: places where people were born, grew up, went to church or school, got married. Visiting family graves need not be a morbid experience especially if you work together tidying up the grave site, placing flowers and telling the story of this person. End the visit by praying together for the deceased family members.

Preparing for transition to secondary school: what does my child need to know?

If your child is going to a Catholic school for the first time it is important that she or he has the basics of what Catholicism is all about.

How are Catholic schools different?

You will have been on open days or school visits, which will give you a starting point. Talk with your child about what he or she noticed about the school and how it might be different from his or her previous experience. You can draw on Chapter 1 to help you discuss this topic. The following are a few suggestions:

- The school brochure: what does your child like and what still seems strange or unknown?

- The mission statement: what does your child think about that and how does he or she feel it will help?

- The school environment: pictures, images, crucifixes, scripture quotes on the walls. Why are these displayed so prominently and how does your child feel about this?

- What the child heard and saw.

What about prayer?

Prayer is at the heart of a Catholic school and takes many forms. Each morning the pupils pray either in their form groups, in year groups or at a whole-school assembly. Their understanding of prayer will be developed through their RE lessons, chaplaincy experiences, school prayer groups and the various liturgies that take place throughout the year. This can seem very strange if prayer has not been part of their life so far. Don't worry: the school is well equipped to help them. However, you as their parents can do much to ensure they don't feel totally at sea. The following are some of the prayers that are most commonly said at some point during the life of the school.

The Our Father

See page 38 above.

The Hail Mary

See page 38 above.

The Glory be

Glory be to the Father,
and to the Son,
and to the Holy Spirit,
as it was in the beginning,
is now and ever shall be,
world without end.
Amen.

Grace before meals

Bless us, O Lord, and these your gifts, which we are about to receive from your bounty, through Christ our Lord. Amen.

Grace after meals

We give you thanks for all your benefits, O almighty God, who lives and reigns, world without end. Amen. May the souls of the faithful departed, through the mercy of God, rest in peace. Amen.

Act of contrition

O my God, I am sorry that I have sinned against you and by the help of your grace I will not sin again. Amen.

The Angelus

Leader: The angel of the Lord declared unto Mary.
Response: **And she conceived by the Holy Spirit.**

Hail Mary…

Leader: Behold the handmaid of the Lord.
Response: **Be it done unto me according to thy word.**

Hail Mary…

Leader: And the Word was made flesh.
Response: **And dwelt among us.**

Hail Mary…

Leader: Pray for us, O Holy Mother of God.
Response: **That we may be made worthy of the promises of Christ.**

Leader: Let us pray.
Pour forth, we beseech thee, O Lord, thy grace into
  our hearts;
that we, to whom the Incarnation of Christ, thy Son,
was made known by the message of an angel,
may by his passion and cross,
be brought to the glory of his resurrection
through the same Christ our Lord.
Amen.

The Apostles' Creed

I believe in God,
the Father almighty,
Creator of heaven and earth;
and in Jesus Christ, his only Son, our Lord,
who was conceived by the Holy Spirit,
born of the Virgin Mary,
suffered under Pontius Pilate,
was crucified, died and was buried;
he descended into hell;
on the third day he rose again from the dead;
he ascended into heaven,
and is seated at the right hand of God the Father
  almighty;
from there he will come to judge the living and the
  dead.

I believe in the Holy Spirit,
the holy catholic Church,
the communion of saints,
the forgiveness of sins,
the resurrection of the body,
and the life everlasting. Amen.

The Nicene Creed

I believe in one God,
the Father almighty,
maker of heaven and earth,
of all things visible and invisible.

I believe in one Lord Jesus Christ,
the Only Begotten Son of God,
born of the Father before all ages.
God from God, Light from Light,
true God from true God,
begotten, not made, consubstantial with the Father;
through him all things were made.
For us men and for our salvation
he came down from heaven,
and by the Holy Spirit was incarnate of the Virgin
  Mary,
and became man.

For our sake he was crucified under Pontius Pilate,
he suffered death and was buried,
and rose again on the third day
in accordance with the Scriptures.
He ascended into heaven
and is seated at the right hand of the Father.
He will come again in glory
to judge the living and the dead,
and his kingdom will have no end.

I believe in the Holy Spirit, the Lord, the giver of life,
who proceeds from the Father and the Son,
who with the Father and the Son is adored and
  glorified,
who has spoken through the prophets.

I believe in one, holy, catholic and apostolic Church.
I confess one Baptism for the forgiveness of sins
and I look forward to the resurrection of the dead
and the life of the world to come. Amen.

The rosary

The websites below will help you to teach your child what the rosary is all about and how to say it. Don't be put off by what appears to be a very complicated way of praying. Begin by looking at a set of rosary beads and explaining how it works and which prayers are said for each bead. The difficult part is explaining how to say the prayers while at the same time meditating or thinking about the particular mystery or story connected with the beads. Once you get the hang of it many young people find it very helpful. You can say one decade or five at a time. However, better to do less well and in a meaningful way than to hurtle through five decades with little meaning. The important thing is to experience praying the rosary as it suits you.

www.familyrosary.org/TheRosary/
HowToPrayTheRosary.aspx

www.beginningcatholic.com/support-files/rosary.pdf

Hail holy Queen

Hail, holy Queen, Mother of Mercy.
Hail our life, our sweetness and our hope.
To thee do we cry, poor banished children of Eve.
To thee do we send up our sighs,
mourning and weeping in this valley of tears.
Turn then, most gracious advocate,
thine eyes of mercy toward us,
and after this our exile
show us the blessed fruit of thy womb, Jesus.
O clement, O loving, O sweet Virgin Mary.
Amen.

Prayer to the Holy Spirit

Come, Holy Spirit, fill the hearts of your faithful and
   kindle in them the fire of your love.
Send forth your Spirit and they shall be created.
And you shall renew the face of the earth.

O God, who by the light of the Holy Spirit did instruct the hearts of the faithful, grant that by the same Holy Spirit we may be truly wise and ever enjoy his consolations, through Christ our Lord. Amen.

Saying prayers is just one way of praying. Prayer can take many forms and your child will be introduced to some of the following types of prayer.

Traditionally, Catholic prayers fall into four types:

- **Adoration:** Praising and giving glory to God.

- **Contrition:** Asking God for forgiveness.

- **Petition:** Asking God for something you need.

- **Thanksgiving:** Saying "thank you", having gratitude in your heart and expressing it.

Each of these types of prayer can be expressed in very creative and contemporary ways. Schools are skilled at finding interesting and meaningful ways of helping young people to be interested in prayer and recognise its importance in their lives.

What celebrations take place in school?

Catholic schools are usually experts in how to celebrate! The most important celebrations in school are the sacraments of the Eucharist (Mass) and reconciliation (confession). The school will also endeavour to support their young people who are receiving the sacrament of confirmation in their parishes. This usually takes place from Year 9 onwards.

If possible each new academic year will begin with the celebration of an academic Mass or a welcome Mass for the new Year 7 pupils. At key times of the year services and celebrations will take place to mark this important time. Penitential services will be organised for all year groups in Advent and Lent. Advent/Christmas plays, carol services as well as the Stations of the Cross all serve to celebrate the Catholic life of the school. Pupils are encouraged to take an active part in their planning as well as their delivery. Year 6 leavers' celebrations will be familiar to all pupils and this is replicated in Years 11 and 13 for the leavers in those year groups. Again it is usually a wonderful celebration of Mass with as many pupils taking an active part in the celebration as possible. Nowadays the American tradition of having a graduation ball has found its way into our secondary schools and sixth form colleges and become our "leavers' ball".

Worship and the liturgical life of the Church

Just as there are different ways of praying, so too there are a variety of ways of entering into worship. Catholic celebrations and worship take different forms, including:

- Liturgy: the official prayers and sacraments of the Church.

- Paraliturgy: this is when the school or parish designs its own style of worship in conformity with the liturgy. Your child will experience these celebrations quite regularly.

- Worship: giving glory, honour, praise and thanks to God.

- Prayer: raising the heart and mind to God, or, simply put, listening and speaking to God, which hopefully will be central to all worship, liturgy and celebrations.

What is the liturgical calendar?

You will notice that your child will make reference to the liturgical life of the Church or liturgical calendar. What the children are discovering are the seasons of the Church's year. This can get complicated. While it may be confusing at first, the result is that no two years will ever look the same – each year has its own unique and colourful pattern of celebration!

When does it begin?

While most people celebrate the New Year on 1 January, the Church's yearly cycle begins in late November or early December, starting on the first Sunday in Advent (the fourth Sunday before Christmas Day).

Advent

Liturgical colour: purple.

Dates: beginning in late November or early December, ending on 24 December.

Advent is a season of preparation to meet Christ, both in the celebration of his birth and in his second coming. People are sometimes surprised to learn that Advent is a penitential season, one that prepares us to stand ready and be prepared for the Lord's second coming. Advent has a strong and positive message. Simply put, the Church is calling us to sort ourselves out. The themes for each week of Advent are: "Wake up!", "Prepare the way of the Lord", "Rejoice" and "Emmanuel is with us".

For Catholics, the call to work for charity and the common good is heightened at times like Advent and Lent (see below). It is a time for personal renewal, growth and transformation. God has heard the cry of those who are poor. Now we must hear this same call to action. Jesus came to save, heal and reconcile – that is a key message of Advent.

Christmas

Liturgical colour: white or gold.

Dates: 25 December to the feast of the Baptism of the Lord (usually the Sunday after Epiphany).

At Christmas Christians celebrate Immanuel, from the Hebrew for "God with us". That, of course, took place in the form of the birth of Jesus. The Christmas season comes to a close after the feast of the Baptism of the Lord, which is usually celebrated on the Sunday after Epiphany. The Epiphany of the Lord is traditionally kept on 6 January and is when Christians celebrate the coming of the magi, or wise men, to worship the infant Jesus. In some countries, including England, Wales and Scotland, the Epiphany is now celebrated on the second Sunday after Christmas. At one time, however, the season lasted for the whole of January and ended with the feast of Candlemas (2 February), which celebrates Jesus being presented in the Temple. So don't be surprised if there are still signs of Christmas when the children return to school after the holiday.

Lent

Liturgical colour: purple.

Dates: from Ash Wednesday (which may occur on any date between 4 February and 10 March) until Easter Sunday, approximately six weeks later.

Lent reminds Christians of the forty days Jesus spent fasting and praying in the desert before he began his ministry (Matthew 4:1-11). It is when the Church prepares for the greatest of all celebrations – Easter. Because its focus is the lead-up to the death of Jesus, Lent is a serious time when the Church encourages us to pray, fast and abstain, and give alms or do something for the good of the community.

Holy Week is the sixth week of Lent, and forms a dramatic climax to the period. It is when Christians focus on the events leading up to the crucifixion of Jesus on Good Friday and the resurrection of Jesus on Easter Sunday. Many schools will organise special penitential services, and re-enactments in the form of passion plays or Stations of the Cross, which represent Jesus' journey to his crucifixion at Calvary.

There are subtle but important variations in the liturgy during Lent. For example, "Alleluia" is not used in worship during Lent – so be careful if you are choosing hymns, and if in doubt ask!

Easter

Liturgical colour: white or gold

Date: Easter Sunday falls on a Sunday between 22 March and 25 April.

This is a time of rejoicing and celebrating Christ's resurrection from the dead. It is about the triumph of good over evil, life over death. The mood is very different – and "Alleluia" is again sung and said. Easter Day leads into Eastertide (Paschaltide), which lasts for fifty days.

Pentecost

Liturgical colour: red

Date: fiftieth day after Easter Day This is another amazing event, when Christians focus on the descent of the Holy Spirit on the apostles (Acts 2:1-12). Red symbolises fire and the Holy Spirit. You may hear Pentecost referred to as Whitsunday, or the birthday of the Church.

Holy days of obligation and other celebrations

The list above outlines the main seasons, feast days, festivals and solemnities that run through the school year. You may also hear talk of holy days of obligation. These are days on which the faithful are obliged to participate in the Mass and to abstain from anything that prevents them from worshipping God. Every Sunday is a holy day of obligation, and some of the other days (such as the feast of the Epiphany on 6 January) are often celebrated on the nearest Sunday. So most of them will not be observed during school time. Occasionally, however, one will, and a Mass will be held at school. In addition, the school will have its own celebrations – such as observing its saint's day – and there may be other local celebrations.

The holy days of obligation are:

- Every Sunday.

- The Nativity of the Lord (Christmas): 25 December.

- The Epiphany of the Lord: 6 January (in England, Wales and Scotland, transferred to the second Sunday after Christmas).

- The Ascension of the Lord: Thursday of the sixth week of Easter (in England and Wales, transferred to the following Sunday).

- The Most Holy Body and Blood of Christ (also known as Corpus Christi): Thursday after Trinity Sunday (in England, Wales and Scotland, transferred to the following Sunday).

- Ss Peter and Paul, Apostles: 29 June (in England and Wales if it falls on a Saturday or Monday it is transferred to the Sunday).

- The Assumption of the Blessed Virgin Mary: 15 August (in England and Wales if it falls on a Saturday or Monday it is transferred to the Sunday).

- All Saints: 1 November (in England and Wales if it falls on a Saturday or Monday it is transferred to the Sunday).

Liturgical colours

This is a very helpful means to knowing which season you are in. In church you will see the sanctuary decoration and the priest's vestments change colour with the seasons. White, red, green, purple and gold are the most common you will see, but black, blue and pink may also be used. If you see red at a time other than Pentecost, it generally means that a martyr or apostle is being commemorated on that day. The third Sunday of Advent is known as "Gaudete" ("rejoice") Sunday, when the penitential purple gives way to rose or pink (rose or pink may be used on the fourth Sunday of Lent, too, which is also Mothering Sunday). This explains why you will see three purple candles and one pink candle around the Advent wreath, with a white candle in the middle.

A lot of the time you will see green. This is the colour for what is known as "ordinary time" and this time links all the other times together.

The sacraments

A sacrament is defined as "an outward sign of inward grace" – the action of God working within someone. The word comes from the Latin *sacramentum*, and came into use in the Church via the Roman army. A recruit became a soldier by taking an oath and being branded! As an initiated soldier, he then had responsibilities, and perks to go with them. This double status provided theologians with the model for what they were trying to illustrate when describing the rites of the Church as both spiritual and physical. The person receiving the sacrament simultaneously assumes new responsibilities and a new spiritual status before God. Happily the practice of branding was never used by the Church!

In the Catholic tradition there are seven sacraments. The first three – baptism, confirmation and Eucharist – are called the "sacraments of initiation", because they are all about entering the Christian community:

- Baptism is where someone (often as a baby) is admitted to the Church. The rite involves the use of prayer; the signing of the cross on the forehead; water, oil, light and a white garment.

- Confirmation is the sacrament that completes baptism; in it the gifts of the Holy Spirit are bestowed upon us.

- The Eucharist, or Holy Communion, or Mass is the sacrament in which Catholics receive the body and blood of Christ. It is seen as an act of unity with the whole Church. Catholics believe that, through a process of transubstantiation, Jesus becomes truly present in the Eucharistic bread (the host or Blessed Sacrament) and the precious blood. In the Catholic tradition it has become normal for people to receive their First Holy Communion before confirmation. However, the ancient order of receiving confirmation first has been reintroduced in some dioceses.

The next two sacraments are called the "sacraments of healing":

- Reconciliation is sometimes called confession or penance, and is when a person confesses his or her sins and is forgiven. Catholics are asked to go to confession at least once a year at or near Easter – hopefully more frequently.

- The sacrament of the sick is given when someone is seriously ill or near death. Formerly this was referred to as the "last rites" or "extreme unction".

Then there are the "sacraments of service and community":

- Matrimony (marriage).

- Holy orders is the ordination of bishops, priests and deacons.

The school is an integral part of the faith community, so it's not uncommon to invite parents, parishioners and friends of the school to share in the celebration.

It is a wonderful testament to the all-embracing nature of the Catholic faith and a demonstration of how life, faith and education are intertwined.

What about RE?

Catholic schools must provide all pupils from the ages of five to sixteen with 10% RE curriculum time. This does not include times of prayer and worship. RE is considered the core of the core curriculum, the most important area of learning in the school. Most Catholic schools also expect their key stage 4 pupils to sit a GCSE in RE. At sixth form level (sixteen- to nineteen-year-olds) the curriculum time requirement is 5% and there is the option of studying RE for those who wish to A Level.

What are retreats?

Schools work hard to offer pupils the opportunity to experience a retreat. This can be a day, in school or away at a retreat or youth centre, or a longer experience of a weekend. Some schools recognise the particular value of this experience and see the difference it can make to pupils and they will offer a week-long programme.

POINTS FOR FAMILY DISCUSSION

▲ Was there anything in this chapter that you did not know before? Share this together.

▲ Do you ever pray together as a family? If not, is this something you might rediscover?

▲ Talk together about how you grew up as a young Catholic or person of a different faith background. How is it different now?

▲ Talk together about your memories of special feast days, religious ceremonies that have played an important part in your life and say why. Look at any pictures of these events together.

▲ Who are the friends and family members that you know may need your prayers and support? Consider creating a family prayer book where you write their names and why you are praying for them. Add in any prayers you would like to write for them.

 Reflection

Lord, you call each of us by name
 to be the best person we can be.
Help us to help one another share
 the fruits of your earth, that
 together we can build a better
 world where each person is
 valued and the gift of your
 creation is a blessing to us all.
Amen. (Claire Bogue/CAFOD)

CHAPTER 4

What difference has being in a Catholic school made to us?

Reflections from pupils

Parents and teachers are very clear about the importance of a Catholic school. However, listening to the views of children and young people is equally important. An adult perspective can sometimes be very different. Head teachers know that the pupil voice is critical to a happy and successful learning environment. I am grateful to pupils from St Anselm's Primary School in Harrow, St Gregory's Sixth Form in Bath and St Mary's Catholic School in Bishop's Stortford for their willingness to take part in these interviews.

Primary school voices – St Anselm's pupil chaplains

Why do you think your families chose St Anselm's for you?

Kya: I think it has to be respect for our religion and to learn as much as we can about it. You are allowed to speak your mind and think for yourself. You also learn to respect other people and their ideas even if you don't always agree, you can still show them respect.

India: I agree and we need to know as much as we can and we do learn a lot here. When I was younger I was not very confident. I am getting much better now. Being a pupil chaplain has helped me a lot.

Niamh: It is also about trying to understand the world. It's God's world and there are so many difficult questions.

Eve: I agree with Niamh but I still have so many things I'm wondering about and that's OK because when you wonder it helps you to work things out.

Aiden: My family wanted me to come here because it is a very good school, the best!

How has this school helped you to develop?

Christopher: Being here has helped me to deal with challenge and to be more forgiving and merciful towards others. When you get someone in your

school who needs help because of their work or behaviour you learn how to help one another. Now I know that if you invite them to play with you and share your friends with them, then they change and become better people. I know if you ask people why they are doing stupid or bad things, then it helps to understand and deal with it or just get over it!

Eve: What I like is this is a place where you can be you and that's OK.

Niamh: Yes, I agree but it also helps us to develop our personalities and find our gifts. Respecting people is very important in our school because we believe that we are all one family and families try to love each other as brothers and sisters.

Tasha: We are trying to follow in the footsteps of Jesus. I enjoy helping the other children learn about the Wednesday Word. This helps us to find happiness. I know that because that's how I feel. I

know Jesus is always there beside me and it makes me very joyful and happy.

Sheremy: I find it difficult sometimes to understand the questions in RE because they are very difficult. Now that I have been chosen as a pupil chaplain I feel more confident to ask and talk about these things. When you do, you find lots of people have the same questions and that is good.

Kya: I agree with Sheremy. In St Anselm's you are encouraged to open up and say what you actually feel. I have come out of my shell and we all have

really. You know Jesus is a good listener, you can feel him listening to your heart.

India: I like being challenged and you are here. It will help us next year in secondary school because we will be used to saying what we think and joining in debates because we are learning how to do that here. I also like it when we teach the younger children about their faith and I would like to take more assemblies.

How do you think St Anselm's is preparing you to understand some of the big issues and challenges in society today?

Christopher: I think this is very important. We have asked our MP to come to St Anselm's because there are lots of things we need to talk to him about. We

are really pleased that he is going to come. But we have also written a letter to tell the Prime Minister what we think and make some suggestions as to how we need to make things better.

Aiden: I am in Year 5 but that should not make any difference. We are all responsible for what happens to the children in our country. I think it is terrible that there are millions of children living in poverty right here.

Niamh: We have to stop being selfish and put ourselves in their shoes.

Tasha: It helps to tell people what is going on and encourage them to help change things. I am more confident now and we are all able to help each other do something.

St Anselm's letter to the Prime Minister

Dear Prime Minister,

We are all pupil chaplains in Year 5 and 6 and we would like to share some of our ideas about what is happening in the country today because it makes us feel very sad. We have learnt two very shocking facts. The first is that there are 3.7 million children living in really bad poverty in the UK. The other fact is that we thought we were one of the richest countries in the world. On the one hand that is good. So why are there so many food banks and people with no homes to live in? Why are there so many buildings that could be homes for refugees and homeless people standing empty?

We are learning that all these big questions are not easy to understand but we feel that it is not good enough for us to say nothing about it.

Prime Minister, could you please tell us why we are still fighting in wars? Violence solves nothing and everyone knows that here. We know people in this country are afraid but we also know that the media does not help by always showing the same terrible pictures over and over again. We feel there is too much greed and leaders who want to dominate and have power over others that they have no right to.

We are a "Rights and Responsibilities School" and proud to be called by this name. However, we are first and foremost a Catholic school where we learn to put ourselves in the shoes of others, to forgive, to share and then there is plenty for everyone.

Please would you do something about advertising? There is far too much pressure on people to buy things they don't want. Especially at Christmastime. What happens? People get all this stuff which they don't need and it just gets stashed under the bed and forgotten. We need much more advertising about looking after each other. The only adverts on TV should be for charities and helping each other. We need to change public attitudes so that everyone is less selfish.

Thank you for reading our letter and we hope you will write back and tell us how we can help you to make our country the best it can be because that is what we are all trying to do. Did you know that Catherine of Siena said, "Be who God meant you to be and you will set the world on fire"? When you are on TV next can you tell everyone that? That is what we at St Anselm's are learning to do.

Thank you for reading our letter and we look forward to hearing from you.

Yours sincerely

Eve, Niamh, India, Christopher, Aiden, Tasha and Sheremy

Reflections from St Gregory's Sixth Form, Bath

The following interviews took place in a coeducational sixth form made up of students from St Gregory's College, Bath. What is interesting about this sixth form is that it draws students who come from a wide range of schools as well as from St Gregory's itself.

Do you feel your Catholic education has prepared you for adult life?

Katie: I think it's encouraged me to think more about others, my place in the world, and be a more active steward of God's creation. I like the values and the ethos of the school. The fact that everyone has mutual respect for everyone, that's what I really like. The standard is high and I wouldn't want to be anywhere else. For me, the basis of RE is really important as I think the concept of respect for different cultures is invaluable. But I think my experience of RE, especially at GCSE, consists of learning a textbook, which seems to devalue the point slightly, but I still think the basis of RE is really, really important. I think our school is very aware of building a Catholic education as we have regular Masses which are respectful and it gives people who don't have the opportunity to go to Mass outside of school the chance to experience that within school.

Josiah: I think it has prepared me well for adult life. It's taught me to be tolerant of different people and their beliefs and shown me how I can integrate Catholic beliefs and Christianity into how I act in daily life because, although we are a Catholic school, and we are taught the pure Catholic messages, it also teaches us how we should act out those messages in our life. Simply put, being kind to other people and being helpful and treating people with respect. So hopefully, although I may not be preaching to people about being Catholic, I hope that just through the way I've learned to act in the environment I've been in, I would be able to be a successful Catholic in my adult life.

I feel it's been very beneficial to me to be educated in a Catholic school. Coming from a Catholic family it's great to feel at one with the process of school like going to Mass and having holy days of obligation, that's a benefit for me. Also, mixing with other people who aren't necessarily Catholics and different religions has also been very interesting and hopefully it has allowed me to be able to openly express my faith, given that we're in a Catholic environment and I don't feel awkward about being a Christian because that is the reason for advertising being a Catholic school. So being a Catholic here doesn't make me feel different. I feel at home and I can tell other people about being a Catholic. There are many students who aren't from a Catholic or Christian background or British and who have parents from different races. Being able to discuss issues with very diverse people and understand their way of thinking is important. Some of my immediate friends are atheists. So being able to debate issues while in a Catholic environment has been good because I can confidently say, I'm a Catholic. So being able to discuss my faith with them and listen to their viewpoints has been very beneficial to me and I think it's enabled me to understand how to develop relationships within a diverse society.

Alexandria: Yes, I feel that Catholic education has given me a good sense of morals and how to deal with difficult situations in an orderly and correct manner, as well as keeping yourself spiritually aware. Catholic schools are stricter than most. Its rules are made on logical and faith decisions which is better because people don't misbehave as much and they learn more. Also, all the spiritual guidance you're given at school which gives you the correct morals and it kind of prepares you for life better because you know more and you know how to deal with things correctly. RE's important because it gives you an insight into other religions and understanding as well as looking into your own and giving explanations for your customs and traditions. I also think I have had a good spiritual education as I've had opportunities to become a

Eucharistic Minister and unique experiences like meeting Bishop Declan through the school by participating in events like Westonbirt Arboretum walk.

Mariya: I agree. It's taught me good morals and helped me to distinguish between right and wrong, based on what the Church teaches. I think it's better to be educated in a Catholic school because students are much better behaved and there's more discipline and the teachers seem to really care about helping students to improve.

Emily, what do you think?

Emily: I feel that I'm more open-minded and I'm able to accept people of all backgrounds because we're growing up in quite a diverse community and my education's taught me to respect other religions as well as other people who don't have religion. I think it's very good because I feel that I can get the support I need because the teachers are more concerned about the students' well-being and their education rather than just facts and figures. Most schools I know in the area are more focused on facts and figures and here it's just a friendlier atmosphere.

I think the standard of education is very high here. It's not forced either. The teachers encourage each individual student to reach their next target or go to the next level and I think mainly it's through the teachers. Also some of the beliefs of Catholics are instilled in the atmosphere and it makes you want to work hard to get the grades you need.

How good do you think your Religious Education has been?

Katie: Within the school I think we're encouraged to think about the importance of sticking to well-guided morals and this helped growing up as I'm more aware of, for example, the fact that a lie is a lie. Even telling a white lie is going against God's will, and I think this triggers a feeling of guilt which I perhaps wouldn't have experienced if I wasn't taught about the importance of morals.

Mariya: I agree with Katie especially now with the refugee crisis and terrorism. I think it's important that kids are taught about other religions and to respect them and not to stereotype. We take moral issues seriously. I find that Catholic schools take issues like bullying a lot more seriously and this is one of the things that helps everyone to feel like they're part of the school and part of the community. We're taught that everyone should be treated equally and that you should love others as you love yourself. We learn to stand up for what we believe in which helps us to stand up for ourselves and others if we think that they've been treated unfairly. One thing that has really helped me was going to Flame 2 because it was a great experience and there was so much energy in the stadium and there were people like Cardinal Tagle and Matt Redman. Friends went from other schools as well.

Josiah: I think RE's very important because in the lower school we learned about the different religions and how to understand them because often before you learn about something like Islam or Hinduism you have a stereotypical image of what it might involve. However, actually learning more in-depth allows you to understand different religions and be more tolerant of them. When we started GCSE we focused more on Catholicism and Christianity and this was equally beneficial. There are many rituals, concepts which I have been putting into practice for many years of my life without fully understanding them. So, through studying Catholicism in RE, I learned to actually understand my own faith in more depth.

Emily: As a subject I think it's very good, especially with the society we're living in because it teaches you about certain religions and their beliefs. We learn about Christians and the different Christian beliefs within certain areas. It also helps some people determine what their religion is, so to speak. Some people feel like their parents are forcing them because they are Catholic. When they come to RE they're really interested in finding out why they are Catholic. This helps them to make an informed choice about what they really believe. Some end up seeing that they don't believe anything. That's just where they are. But it helps them to be a better person in the future, so they finally know who they are. We go on lots of retreats. In Year 8 we went to Ammerdown and we were able to do meditation there and painting rocks. We were also taught how to find peace and respect for each other.

What has had the greatest impact on you as a member of the school community, and why?

Katie: The greatest impact on me has been when I went on the Borneo trip in the summer and that was absolutely amazing, it was literally the best experience of my life. We did do a community project and we were helping build a church and so it was relevant! It was so good and it was getting to see the different ways that people worshipped and it just had a massive impact on me because they were so dedicated and amazing with what they had, which is so little compared to what I have. I think that has had the most impact on me.

Josiah: I'd have to say it's the encouragement of my teachers to see me achieve my best because they've always been encouraging and pushed me to achieve more and more as I've gone through the school. There hasn't really been a point when I've thought that they didn't believe in me. Just having that encouragement has helped me to achieve a lot. I'm very proud of what I've achieved and I think lots of that is due to the encouragement I've received and how kind my teachers have been to me. The relationship I've had with my teachers has been great.

What about prayer?

Alexandria: Throughout my education I've been encouraged to pray deeply and meaningfully. Lower years are encouraged to pray though song and rhymes which always reminded me to pray in thanks as well as in need like in times of emergency.

Josiah: Yes, I think from Year 7 we were always taught to say grace before we go to lunch and they do that in a very accessible manner. I remember saying grace to the tune of the *Addams Family*, which I won't repeat now, but it got everyone involved and everyone was happy to pray, even if they weren't necessarily Christian. Then as you move through the school the prayers have become more sophisticated and often they give you the choice to just pray for what you want and it's not as enforced but it is encouraged to do that. Through Masses it's good to have that time of reflection to be able to think about the Gospels.

Emily: In RE lessons sometimes we're taken to the chapel. I do have to say, sometimes the chaplain did give us sweets at the end because we were so good. They taught us how to do meditation and how we should pray and respect others when they're praying, because in assembly sometimes some people are praying and others aren't but we've learned to respect that other people are praying silently.

Do you think your schooling has helped to prepare you for the many moral and justice issues in society?

Emily: I think a lot of my morals have come from school because in PSHE [Personal, Social and Health Education] lessons we talk about what you should do and what not to do in certain situations and I think it's helped me focus on my education more and stay away from certain things, such as drugs and drink, and more dangerous situations that are coming about more and more in society. Drugs and alcohol are increasing in youths but I think because we've been more aware of what we're told, and the implications it has, it's better for us.

Josiah: I guess it comes back to the RE GCSE again because within that we learned about issues such as abortion and contraception and euthanasia and really understanding and being able to empathise with the issues. We had class debates which increased my awareness of how other people think and allowed me to empathise with them and also develop my own opinion further as opposed to just agreeing with it because I know that's what I should either agree or disagree with. Knowing the reasons behind it and being able to reason with other people's viewpoints has really helped me develop my understanding and hopefully, when faced with moral issues in later life, I will be able to implement some of the things I've learned and be more understanding and empathetic with other people.

I feel that through being here I've been able to identify injustice a lot more than I would have been able to before. Through looking at these issues in subjects like geography, we recognise the disparity between the high-income and the low-income areas, as well as the north–south divide of the globe. So learning about these issues has enabled me to understand that they're wrong. We can do something about them and hopefully in my later life I'll be able to challenge effectively and be part of the change. If I see someone doing something which isn't right, I will have the confidence to challenge the injustice.

Alexandria: In all schools there are obviously groups of friends and they don't always get along and turning the other cheek or sometimes just protecting a friend is the best thing. Sometimes teachers give you support for trying to do the right thing which is the best thing possible. It's helped me gain confidence.

When I first started this school I had a very bad stutter and through my friends, the chapel, through teachers, I lost my stutter and I now have confidence and I think I could stand up to anyone if they were doing something that was an injustice.

How do you feel about church?

Alexandria: Being here has helped because we have regular Masses at school. We're given reminders about things that we should do and it has brought me closer to the Church rather than drawing me away from it. I see how it can be part of my everyday life and it's like a reminder that everything I do is in the eyes of God. Having access to the chapel has helped me a great deal.

It has given me a place where I can go where there's people I can trust and everyone gets along and it's an opportunity where I can express myself and no one will judge me but also it's peaceful. The most important thing is, God is there. I always feel his presence in the chapel and it's a place where I can go when I just need to be alone or I need to speak with people. It has definitely given me more courage and I feel more comfortable around other people now.

Josiah: I agree with the others. As I previously mentioned, RE has allowed me to understand many of the concepts and rituals and the way things were set up and helped me to understand my faith in more depth. Through what I've been taught in school and being in an environment where I am able to practise. Going to holy days of obligation wasn't something I'd done previously, although I think my father did. Whereas being at school that means I was able to attend those days too and understand their significance.

View from the Hodgson brothers

Two brothers, Dominic, aged ten, and John, aged sixteen, attend Catholic schools in Bishop's Stortford in Hertfordshire.

Dominic will follow his brother John into the same comprehensive school, St Mary's, in the autumn. The boys clearly enjoy being at their schools and are doing well. However, they raise some really challenging issues for both schools and parents.

Dominic, how do you feel about being in St Joseph's?

Dominic: I like the fact that we all try to live the same beliefs and values. Our mission statement – "To live, love and learn in a caring Christian community" – helps us all stay focused and aiming for the same thing.

I am surprised you started with your school mission statement.

Dominic: We all do that because it is what we are about and what we believe. It is a leveller in a way. We all stick to it, well most of us do. A few people think they are clever or cool and say they don't, but I think that's because of what's going on outside school really. People my age are seeing and playing with stuff way beyond their ages and it has a bad impact on their lives and the way they think. They can't handle it really.

John: Technology is impacting in a much greater way than most adults realise. Dominic's age group are exposed to things that people my age would never have been and that's just five years ago. Take a phone. Parents buy phones that have web access for their children, because they are cheaper than ones that don't. What they don't think enough about is what their children will do with these phones. The peer pressure is considerable and most parents never check up anyway. I would honestly say that my life experience was nearer my parents' experience when I was Dominic's age than his is now. They are just light years apart and it is getting more so every year.

Dominic, how does your being in a Catholic school help you as a person?

Dominic: I like the fact that we are challenged to do our best. The teachers will give you things to make you think and although they help they push you to work it out for yourself. I am glad the work is hard otherwise it would be boring. In our school you will always be challenged to go higher. It can be difficult for some children, but we help them and I like that. Sometimes I am asked to work with children who are struggling and I think that is important. They also help me too with things I can't do. I like the fact that we are a community with the same ambitions and values which bind us together.

What do you think, John?

John: I agree. The two schools are very similar. Our mission statement is "A Catholic community dedicated to achieving excellence for all" and I think that is true. We receive a well-rounded education with a strong emphasis on Christian beliefs and moral values. This comes through in all our subjects. We are a socially diverse community though not so culturally so. That is a shame really because you don't mix with many people who reflect the broader society we live in. But you can't change the mix of the area really.

How well do you think you are being prepared for the next stage in your life?

Dominic: I will be sad to leave because I have been here since I was two years old in preschool. I am excited about going to my next school because I feel ready for the challenge.

John: I want to stay on in the sixth form. I think it has been pretty good so far. You are encouraged to think for yourself and most teachers are happy to be challenged by their students. It can be difficult for some teachers in a Catholic school when ethical issues come up and students start debating them because I think some teachers may feel that they are not sure what they can say from a Catholic perspective especially if the student really knows their theology or more than they do on the topic. I am really grateful that my education has not just been grades-driven. Some of my friends in other schools clearly suffer from this. Nothing else matters but getting the best grades so the school looks good in the league tables. It is not like that in St Mary's.

We are expected to be the very best we can be, but there is more to life than just exam results. That is what I mean by a rounded education which is what you need today. Things are changing so fast.

To what extent do you think your Religious Education has helped you?

Dominic: At the moment we are learning about being a sacramental people. At first it is hard, but I think it really means seeing how God is working through me, like when I stand up for a friend who is having difficulty. It is about seeing how the sacraments are stepping stones, a bit like targets to aim for really. They help us to follow the right path all your life.

John: I really enjoy it and want to do A level Religious Studies. I think it is important because it gives you a way of making sense of life and engaging with the questions so many people have today. It sets your learning in a context and helps to consolidate everything. We are encouraged to ask questions and think for ourselves which is important especially if you go to university where you will meet people with different views. I feel I will be able to handle that. Going back to the social media and the internet I think this is having a big impact on the way we learn. We can find out just about anything but what we need to know is how to make sense of it and if it is really true. That is where our school is very good. We are not empty minds to be filled up. We need to be taught how to deal with so much information that it can get really confusing. I am looking forward to the sixth form because you have more freedom to learn on your own.

Clearly you both enjoy and appreciate your schools. Is there anything that you think would improve them further?

Dominic: I wish we could do something about what parents let their children see and play with. There are so many violent video games that are way above the age limit of our school and so many pupils are playing them because they put pressure on their parents and they give in. I would like to see the school helping parents to stop this. It would help them to be better in school too. I am also on our chaplaincy team and that is great, but it would be even better if we could do more things besides raising money, which we are really good at.

John: We are an outstanding school so this is difficult. One thing I would like is to see more of the governors. I know they come into school but it would be good if we knew them all and discussed things together. I know this is not easy to arrange, but we could learn a lot from each other.

Would you send your children to a Catholic school?

Dominic: Yes, because they are the best!

John: I agree if the Catholic school was the best in the area. I can see the difference between our school and other schools through my friends.

POINTS FOR FAMILY DISCUSSION

- ◭ What do you think about what the children from St Anselm's said?
- ◭ The Hodgson brothers raise some important points about the exposure of young people today and the media. Do you feel this could be better controlled within the family?
- ◭ How did you feel about the responses from the sixth-form students?
- ◭ How do the responses from all the children reflect your experiences at school?
- ◭ Have the responses from any of the pupils challenged you as parents? If so, how?

 Reflection

We leave this place, Lord,
inspired by your Word,
challenged by your example,
empowered by your Spirit.
Give us the strength to be people
who inspire others with your Word,
challenge others with your example
and empower others with your Spirit.
Amen. (Mo Baldwin/CAFOD)

CHAPTER 5

Will a Catholic education help my child in the world of work?

Parents are rightly concerned that the choice of school will give the best possible education and enable their child to secure meaningful employment. Let us look again at how well Catholic schools actually perform compared to other schools. The following website will give you the most up-to-date information each year. Follow the CES Census link: **www.catholiceducation.org.uk/**

At the end of Catholic primary education

At age eleven, Catholic schools outperform the national average English and Maths SATs scores by 6%.

Ofsted findings

83% of Catholic secondary schools have Ofsted grades of good or outstanding (75% nationally).

GCSE

At GCSE, Catholic schools outperform the national average by 5%.

Contrary to some political opinions that are promoted, Catholic schools are a great success story. This is not just in academic achievement but also in all other areas of the students' education and development. Catholic schools (with a few exceptions) are at least as good as other schools and in most cases better.

Voices from the workplace

The following interviews have been conducted with employers and people in the world of work who are also responsible for recruiting staff into their firms.

Mr Patrick O'Dowd – Director of Administration and Personnel

How did your education help you for your role today?

I find this a hard question to answer because I am not sure if it was the school or my experience of the parish. In primary school it really did prepare me for secondary school and I had a strong sense of belonging to a community. Our priest played a key role in this. In fact he was fantastic! When I went to secondary school it was different. However, the opportunities were there for doing things in school but I was not always that interested probably because there was so much going on outside. As teenagers you don't always see the connection between school and parish. Now I can see that the school and the parish worked closely and I and many other young people like me had opportunities to get involved in a social life, pastoral outreach like Lourdes pilgrimages and activities outside school. Most of my friends also went to a Catholic school so this helped. I think that is important. We became very active and this widened our horizons. I think a Catholic school must be ambitious for the higher gifts. Catholic schools really focus on the dignity of the human person and I think that is very important in the workplace.

How did these experiences impact on your role today?

Working is more than having a job. It has to make a difference. As a person in a management position, responsible for a large number of people, I really understand the importance of ensuring that all staff know that they are equally important and matter to the organisation. They need to experience this care and respect. I think that people in management positions must not look for an employee who will simply fulfil their role but look deeper for their potential and help them to develop and grow.

When you are interviewing, what do you look for?

Well, naturally that they have the right skills, experience and fit the job description. But yes, for me I am looking for something more in a person. I sit through a multitude of interviews. Most applicants have the basics to fit the role, but I want to see if that person will be capable of representing the best interests of the organisation. Do they have that something extraordinary?

So what is that something extraordinary?

It is hard to quantify, but I look to see if this candidate will build and contribute to the community at work and outside. Do they have an awareness of the bigger picture?

Would you say there is a difference between an applicant who has been educated in a Catholic school and one who has not?

In most cases, yes. They have a broader understanding and sense of who they are. So whatever they are applying for they want to be the best they can be. Very often I find that someone who is in a job that some might argue is not very important becomes a really key individual and one who brings a sense of community and care to the organisation. A people person who notices and shows it too. I have noticed that many young people who apply here bring a real sense of respect for themselves and others. They are usually very hard-working and want to please.

Are there areas where you feel schools could do more to prepare young people for the workplace?

That's difficult because students leave school at either sixteen or eighteen, then go to college or university, so it can be a long time before they appear in this office. But yes, I think more can be done and not just in schools but all through higher education. One area I think Catholic schools could work on is helping their young people to know how to challenge appropriately. A good company is looking for innovation, creativity and growing their own leaders.

There is a wonderful quote from Pope John Paul II in *Laborem Exercens* when he says that people in the workplace must:

> *assist one another to live holier lives. In this way the world will be permeated by the spirit of Christ and more effectively achieve its purpose in justice, charity and peace… Therefore, by their competence in secular fields and by their personal activity, elevated from within by the grace of Christ, let them work vigorously so that by human labour, technical skill and civil culture, created goods may be perfected according to the design of the Creator and the light of his word*
>
> Laborem Exercens 25

Isn't that a bit idealistic for today's world, Patrick?

Not at all. This is why we are here. Work is for making the world a better place for everyone. Sadly this is not always the case and that is the special contribution of a Catholic education. It is the "why" we do what we do as well as the "what" we do.

Mrs Angela Williams – Senior Administrator

In your experience do you find applicants for posts from Catholic schools any different from applicants from other schools?

Skillswise, I would have to say not really. As important as skills are, I want more than that.

What are you looking for?

In this job you have to have excellent people skills and an awful lot of patience and understanding. You are dealing with the public and at times they can be very challenging. Sometimes you have to just knock them over with kindness and charm! I am looking for a person with a high level of respect, even when the going gets tough. They must be a team player and form good relationships.

Wouldn't you get that with any good person?

Yes, you would. But as I said, I want to appoint team members who are naturally sensitive towards others, especially to the poor and vulnerable. We see that quite often and what people need is help and understanding. In this line of work you have to often "go the extra mile" and you're not paid for that either. But that is what makes this work so rewarding. Helping someone who is really in need and at times at the end of their tether. It does not help to just pass them on or say, "I can't help you." We need to make sure we do help even if it is identifying that person for them if we don't know what to do. And I like my team to follow up, making sure that the problem is solved or at least they are getting the right help.

Aren't you asking rather a lot? After all, they are not paid to "go the extra mile".

I don't think so. We are a service and that's what makes it so. I find that we get a lot of applicants for posts here from Catholic schools because of where we are situated. These schools educate their students to a high level in social justice and social care. Their CVs often show a wide range of activities for the good of the community and care for people in need. It's awareness and service for the greater good. That's essential here. However, there are youngsters from other schools who are naturally that way, so I can't say only students who come from a Catholic school would have these qualities, it is just that we see more of it from these schools.

Would you say that young people today are too compliant and just do their job?

Some are. We try to weed them out at interview because that is not good enough here. We want independent thinkers – polite ones, mind you – and people who will step up and take responsibility.

Mr John Corrigan – Property Manager

As a property manager you work with a very wide range of people. To what degree do you think having a Catholic education makes any difference?

Well, my view on the importance of having a Catholic education has been greatly influenced by the fact that I am now the chair of governors of a large Catholic college. Naturally I want to employ and work with people I can trust, who have integrity and are good at what they do.

So how does your college prepare young people for the world of work?

To be honest I have to say that I have had my eyes opened. I used to think that it was a matter of just getting the best grades, going to university and then hopefully getting taken on by a good firm. Now I see it very differently. All those things matter, but there is a lot more to it than that. The governors and I are in the process of evaluating just this question. How well are we preparing our young people for the world of work so that they can make a difference? I do notice that there is a marked difference between young apprentices which does point to their schooling. Catholic schools are well known for inspiring young people to have a very serious work ethic which is highly focused and disciplined. All workers want to know why they are doing something, so you are not just a chippy, or a plumber, you're part of the team creating something really useful and important and hopefully beautiful as well.

Are you saying you want people of vision?

Yes, I am. You might argue that in my industry the people on the ground just need to stick to the plans and get on with it. But that is a very narrow view. It is important that someone in my position listens carefully to the ideas and insights of all the team. Very often it is people on the shop floor who have the best solutions to problems.

How well do you think Catholic schools prepare their students for leadership roles?

Just recently I was at a presentation by the senior prefects to the governing body. I have to be honest and say that we were all amazed. The confidence and clarity of their vision and suggestions was very impressive. They were undaunted at facing the whole governing body and nothing phased them. I am sure that I was not that confident at their age. I can honestly say that our school turns out highly confident and competent young adults who are creative and full of ideas.

How well do you think Catholic schools equip young people with a sense of values that are able to stand the pressure of the prevailing liberal culture?

Of course, this varies with the individual and the influence from home. But it is true to say that in the main our young people have wider interests. As governors we are keen to hear about how students are being educated about social justice issues and the dignity of the human being. Relationships are very important in my line of work. So a respectful and listening ear is essential. We are there to help people realise their hopes and dreams for a project, so we need to be aware of why we are there. Of course money matters but I want to employ and work with people who have a bigger vision.

Do you see many like this?

It is mixed, of course, but the last interview we held was really encouraging. The field was very strong and they all came from very varied backgrounds. Each candidate demonstrated a strong work ethic and seemed to have the necessary skills. However, one young man really stood out. Great attitude towards work and why he wanted the job. His ability to actually make the links between his values and his work was exceptional. He had all the skills you might expect, naturally he had a lot to learn too, but he was open and ready to learn. That's what makes the difference in who you choose. Whatever your beliefs and values they do manifest themselves in what you do.

Did he get the job?
You bet he did!

Dr Elizabeth Quarterman – GP

In your view as a doctor, would having a Catholic education make a difference?

Definitely. I think one of the "benefits" of faith is that you don't have to worry about not knowing things, the Great Unknowns, because you have a belief that everything does ultimately hold together and God at least knows that, even if you don't! For me as a doctor, this is very important, because patients expect you to have answers. Naturally, there is much we do know about the human person but there are many more questions than answers. So I think, with hindsight of course, that this is one of the benefits of a Catholic education. So much of life is in fact mystery.

There are those who feel a Catholic education is too narrow a perspective on life. What do you think?

I can only speak from my experience. I think it is very powerful to be at a school where every so often you can go to Mass, or when some of the teachers would start every lesson with a Hail Mary or a prayer. You become aware that, whatever your status, we were all part of something larger than the school. Quite startling sometimes, to see a teacher – who might have been telling you off – go up to communion in the same queue that you did! There is nothing narrow at all about Catholic education because at its best it teaches you how to think and question life. Also Catholic schools have pupils from all walks of life, nationalities and backgrounds. I'd say it was quite the opposite really.

What would you say is the most significant contribution that a Catholic education makes to young people today?

It is hard to identify one thing as I think there are many. Looking back, I think the idea that, although grades are important, education is not all about marks, but doing and being the very best you can be as a human being. Therefore getting good marks is part of *that*, rather than your worth depending primarily on your marks. I remember that it did affect my career choice, in that, ambition aside, my education did foster a sense of thinking about the future – my decisions and choices – in terms of "vocation" rather than just a job. This definitely gives one a strong sense of significance, of value, of responsibility. I notice that in some of our young trainee medics coming through and I rejoice in the fact that the more selfish side of society has not defeated what I consider to be extremely important in medicine.

Is there something that you personally are thankful for, having been educated in Catholic places of learning?

Looking back – so many memories! – I think it does give you a kind of security, because it's the same world and much the same values and attitudes that inform one's home life, so I think as a start in life it's invaluable. I think if you don't have an initial level of security, it's very hard to be accepting of diversity later. Anxiety can make people defensive, prejudiced and suspicious. I think it certainly solved one problem for me before it could even become a problem. I'm sure the experience of doing all my chemistry, biology, physics exams in that setting meant it was never a problem for me to hold faith and science together as one discipline informing another long before I could

have articulated an argument about it. Some things, maybe the most important things, are learnt by personal experience rather than out of books.

Mr James Duffy – Project Administrator

James, having been to Catholic schools until you were eighteen years old, how do you feel your education has helped to prepare you for adult life?

I find it hard to answer that question as for me the greatest influence on my life has come from my family. I suppose my schools reinforced our family values and beliefs. In school it was more like a subliminal message that kept running through everything else. Looking back on my life since I left school I can see that the choices I have made are because of my culture and beliefs.

To what extent did your education help you find what you want to do?

To be honest, on one level it hasn't. I initially wanted a career in medicine. I have spent nearly two years working in a hospital and I loved it. The hours were challenging, but when you are there, even if it is Christmas Day, you can make a real difference to someone's life. The values that you have been brought up with and taught at school really come into play. But to be honest the hours and lack of time for other things has really made me question if this is the life I want to live. You must be truly committed to the lifestyle the vocation entails. I suppose you could say what I learnt at school has shown me that there is more to life than just work.

Were you challenged to think for yourself at school?

Looking back, I would say yes. As I said before, school builds on family values. We did a lot of charity work which most people really got stuck into. I did and I found it motivated me to ask questions and want to do something to make a difference. We were encouraged to question. I would describe it as up until Year 11, you are putting your kit on, warming up, but it was not until Years 12 and 13 that you play the game.

So where do think you will go now?

I am working in a graphic design company at present and it is very interesting. I am learning a lot. Ultimately, I just don't know. Business can be very selfish, for many it is all about the company with little or no consideration for the common good. I hope I can find the right work for me which combines a balanced lifestyle and being able to make a difference, like medicine, teaching or law. What I do know is, I will end up in a more vocational rather than pure business field.

Do you think it is possible today to find just the right job?

I hope so. What I do know is that it will be the one that helps me to be the person I want to be. The dilemma for me is trying to balance what my heart wants, the brain and the demands of a job.

Did you find it difficult to reconcile personal beliefs and values when working in the hospital?

No, I didn't, because I was never in a really controversial situation. However, you do notice how quickly you empathise with patients in distress or need. I suppose that comes from training at school

and home, because you are really forced to think about others with respect and sensitivity. Thinking back, I did have a lot of exposure to people in need, the poor and the marginalised.

Would you send your child to a Catholic school?

Only if it was the best school for them and by that I mean that it gives the best all-round joined-up experience.

Hannah – Radio Producer

How do you think you have benefited from a Catholic education?

I think I benefited from a Catholic education because I have a stronger understanding of the teaching of the Catholic Church and also of the biblical basis of the faith and of Christianity as a whole. I think that the negative side was that we didn't learn as much about other religions as a child would at a non-faith school. That's a shortcoming in a multicultural society.

To what extent do you think your education has impacted on the way in which you approach your work?

I think the main example of my education influencing my work is when I've worked on programmes with a religious angle. It has given me a knowledge base to draw on, particularly about biblical references. I think it has also meant I've been more drawn to religious topics when I develop ideas for programmes. Interestingly, these aren't always Christianity-based ideas – my interest is in religion and faith in general.

In your work as a radio producer do you notice a difference between those who have been educated in a faith context and those who have not?

Generally I can't distinguish those who have been to a faith school. The exception to this is if we are working on a religious or spiritual programme, when sometimes it's clear that some people's frame of reference is different, due to their education.

Would you recommend that your friends send their children to a Catholic school?

I would recommend Catholic education for the reasons outlined in my first answer, and also because I think it helps to foster a strong sense of identity and community, which is very important later in life – it makes you feel part of the local Catholic community while you're at school, but also when you move into the wider world you're still tied to a Catholic community. My reservation would be about the lack of diversity in the school. At my school, there were no non-Catholic pupils at all. I met people of other faiths outside school, but I think if a child didn't have that contact with other sorts of people it wouldn't be very healthy.

Mr Andel Singh – Solicitor Advocate and Barrister (Criminal)

What do you look for in someone wanting to train for the legal profession?

There are various routes in. I am always happy to have young people from sixteen to nineteen years old on work experience. This can give them a really good insight into what the profession is like. We also have apprentices who take a longer route into law, working and studying at the same time, which can be less expensive. Then of course there are those who come in from university. Naturally they need to have the academic ability to cope with the demands of the profession, but for me that is not the most important aspect. We are always looking for someone who has a wider perspective on life and is able to see beyond the immediate situation. Integrity, honesty and empathy are all very important in our work. Working in the justice system means long hours and the need to have a disciplined mind.

Does coming from a faith background make a difference?

That is an interesting question because most of the people I work with are from faith backgrounds. As far as having a good work ethic goes, I would say there is little difference and I would also say that there is a similar level of empathy. What is noticeable is the level of self-discipline that young trainees from Catholic schools have. They also tend to be very respectful of others and want to help those in difficulty. They have a real sense of responsibility for the common good.

Do you think they have had sufficient training at school to prepare them for the world of work?

In many ways the answer would be yes. They are ready to learn. If I had a criticism it would be the need to develop their analytical skills further in order to engage with the complexity of some cases they will be dealing with. Young Catholics tend to be very good on the "what" of a situation, but not so good on the "how" and the "why". As a Catholic myself, I am not sure why this is. I notice that those coming from Catholic establishments are well able and confident to ask questions without fear, so it does seem to be something of a contradiction.

Might it be the way they are taught the curriculum in schools today?

Yes, and this would apply to all schools. I think Catholic schools are well placed to help their students think more critically and look for the links and connections that help us to understand a situation beyond the immediate information before them.

What percentage of young people come into your firm because they want to make a difference, or are there other reasons?

The majority for the same reasons that I did. You want to help and make a difference to people's lives. This is encouraging. You may find yourself working with a family spanning several generations. On one level that can be disheartening, but what I see is that although you may not be able to stop the tendency to offend from one generation to the next, you can at least advise and try and minimise the damage because you form a relationship of trust with the family and that counts for a great deal.

To what extent might your own views of morality and the law conflict?

This is where it can get difficult. You have to keep to a very strict professional code and approach. At the end of the day we are there to uphold the law and protect society in doing so. However, learning to reconcile one's own views and the requirements of the job can be challenging, especially when you are representing someone who has broken the law but you know that the circumstances of their life are such that they had little option. A good example of this is a single mother who has no more money and steals to feed her child. It happens.

The challenge for me is to represent this mother in such a way that she, though guilty, is helped to bring up her child and stay out of trouble. It is even more difficult when you are representing a client who has no apparent reason or excuse for breaking the law. Here the objectivity comes in. Look beyond and outside everything you have before you. "What is the truth?" is the big question before all of us. When it is really difficult I will seek the advice of other colleagues. Many minds are better than one.

I see that you are also an advocate.

Yes. I really enjoy this work and want to take it further.

Has this option been influenced by your Catholic background?

Yes. Very much so. Particularly advocacy for the poor and the marginalised in society. This was part of my education at home and in school. So it is not surprising that I should want to take this up. I have always been interested in this field of work and had to make the difficult decision of turning down the opportunity of training to become a judge. If I had gone down this route, as prestigious as it appears, it would have meant losing the personal contact and relationship with my clients. I did not want to sacrifice this side of my work.

From your experience of interviewing young people wanting to go into the legal profession, what advice would you give them?

That is a hard one! The main thing is, know why you want to do this. You have to come at it from a standpoint of deep conviction. The training is tough and expensive, but if it is what you really want then keep going and don't give up.

Mr Seamus English – Senior Relationship Bank Manager

In your experience of recruiting new staff what do you look for?

It is no secret that the banking business has been through a very rough time and we are not out of the woods yet. The disgraceful events of the past few years have deeply affected everyone in finance and it would be true to say that many people feel tarred with the same brush. You cannot turn a blind eye when things are going wrong. This is what happened at the highest levels right across the industry. I know I, for one, took what has happened quite personally. I am in a service industry and relationships and trust are everything. This is what I look for in my team and any deviation from that is totally unacceptable. If I am honest I find the corruption and greed very hurtful, not to mention shameful.

Have the events of the past few years altered your choice of colleagues?

As I said, everything is built on trust in my business. Integrity must be without question. When I am involved in the selection process for new team members I look very carefully at references and what other professionals say about them. So yes, it has.

It can't be easy coping with the tensions within banking at this present time so how do you maintain a team ethic and what values do you look for?

We have to focus on building trust and remember that we are a service. We have revisited our values and now strive to uphold them at all times. For us the customer is key. Our friends and family and theirs too are important. We must always build trust in all our relationships within the team and with the customer. Central to all we do is, keep it simple. No hidden anything. What you hear and see is what you get. We strive to fulfil our ideal that we are better together and very important too is that in all our undertakings we seek to empower one another and our clients to be and do what they are aiming for.

There is a lot in those values. To what extent do people seeking to work in your bank share those values?

There is a lot of work to be done to ensure that these values really do impact on our service. Every member of the team has to feel that this is really what they believe. Otherwise it is false and the customer picks that up very quickly. If people are from a background where beliefs and values inform what they do and who they are, then it permeates through.

In looking at references and CVs do you think it makes a difference if they have attended a Catholic school?

Well, we don't talk about religion as such, but yes, in my experience it does. As a firm we have embarked on the values agenda because the recent past shows what happens if you don't. It is true that you are what you believe. It is not essential to have a Catholic education, of course not, but when you have been educated with a strong sense of right and wrong, have a high level of self-discipline and are striving for the common good, then that is what is going to make a difference to your work. This is what the banking industry urgently needs.

Has the values agenda made any recognisable difference on a daily basis?

Very much so. There are clear parameters now and the articulation of a company value culture has made a big difference. There has to be a common vision and way of doing things. We are all focused on the "how" we interact, not the "what".

What have you noticed, if anything, that stands out from team members who have had a Catholic schooling?

They often have a high level of integrity and genuinely do want to go above and beyond what is expected. This makes it much easier for us to mould them into a member of the team. I often find that they have had a wide experience of working for charitable projects and social issues. This immediately interests me and that is what I ask them to talk about at interview. In this way you get a better picture of what they are really like as a person.

Do you share your values with interviewees?

Very much so and I want to hear their responses too. How they see these panning out in their daily work. Usually people applying for a job in this bank are highly qualified, and have usually been to university. However, it is sometimes good to go straight in from school and train on the job. It can be better for us too because then we are not undoing ridiculous expectations just because they have got a degree. I spent twenty years in education and for the most part it was a very good education, but was I trained to use it? That is the question.

What would you say to a young person thinking of getting into finance today?

As I said, get involved in other things before you leave school or college. Widen your horizons and get some life experience. Make sure your motives are right. Being in finance is not just about earning a good wage. Yes, it is important, but it is a service and one that must serve not exploit. I interview applicants with lists of A grades, well done, but what else is there in your life, is what I want to know. What do you think and care about? What are your values?

POINTS FOR FAMILY DISCUSSION

- Did any particular comment strike you from one of the interviews? Why?
- What did you find interesting from the interviews?
- As a result of reading this chapter, how important do you consider the choice of school to be for your child's future?
- Do you think a Catholic school would be more able to prepare your child for adult life?
- Do any members of your family recognise the importance of the values expressed in this chapter in their workplace?

 Reflection

Lord, we give thanks for the gift of work. May we use it to continue to do your work to make this a better and more just world where all are treated with dignity and respect. May we never lose sight that yours, O Lord, is the greatness and the power and the glory and the majesty and the splendour, for everything in heaven and earth is yours. Wealth and honour come from you; you are the ruler of all things. Now, our God, we give you thanks, and praise your glorious name. Everything comes from you, and we have given you only what comes from your hand. Amen. (based on 1 Chronicles 29:11-14)

CHAPTER 6

Expectations of parents and carers of children in Catholic schools

What the Church asks of parents

The Church takes education of the young very seriously. We see in Canon Law the requirement of parents and carers to educate their children and to take great care in how this is done because children need to receive their full entitlement as young Catholics growing up in their faith and traditions. However, it is not just the responsibility of parents. The whole community is called upon to assist in the process of educating young people.

> **Can. 796 §1** *Among the means of advancing education, Christ's faithful are to consider schools as of great importance, since they are the principal means of helping parents to fulfil their role in education.*[1]

The Education Act of 1944 gave the Catholic community the right to educate its children according to their beliefs and values. The whole community sprang into action, raising the money to build schools to provide a place for every Catholic child. This was a very ambitious aim. The story of the building of Catholic maintained schools in the UK is an amazing one! At parish level, families worked together raising the money and often the workforce to build schools regardless of whether they had children of school age or not. Why? Because they recognised that without a Catholic education the Catholic community would not flourish and be able to take their place in society and bring about the changes that were so urgently needed for the good of all people.

This has been a wonderful success story. Catholics are now represented at every level in society. The downside of the success story has been the inevitable reality that with success comes affluence and choice. For a whole host of reasons the vast majority of Catholics pay scant attention to the practice of their faith or attend church. Yet the majority are very serious about getting their child educated in a Catholic school. This seems a strange contradiction. Surely, one might think, if people were not serious about their faith, then why would it matter to them if their children went to a Catholic school? Clearly it is not as straightforward as that. While many Catholic families rarely, if ever, attend church they still feel that they are Catholic and that is a good thing. Therefore deep inside them is the desire to do the very best they can for their children. Very often this means a Catholic education.

---

[1] All quotations from Canon Law are taken from The Canon Law Society of Great Britain and Ireland, *The Code of Canon Law* (London: Collins, 1983).

Pope Francis, recognising this situation, called on all who are responsible for bringing up children to reclaim their responsibility as Catholic families when he said:

It is time for fathers and mothers to return from their exile – for they have exiled themselves from bringing up their children – and to fully resume their educational role.

General Audience, 20 May 2015

It is true that there are cases where it is not in the child's best interests to attend the local Catholic school. In these instances it is very important that parents take the religious education and formation of their children seriously and do not just fall back on the excuse, "We go to Mass on Sunday" and that's the beginning and end of it!

Can. 793 §1 *Parents, and those who take their place, have both the obligation and the right to educate their children. Catholic parents have also the duty and the right to choose those means and institutes which, in their local circumstances, can best promote the catholic education of their children.*

Parents do know what is best for their children and the Church recognises this responsibility.

Can. 798 *Parents are to send their children to those schools which will provide for their catholic education. If they cannot do this, they are bound to ensure the proper catholic education of their children outside the school.*

Some parishes have classes for children who have not been able to get into a Catholic school, or for whom the local Catholic school does not meet their particular needs. In these cases it is the responsibility of parents to educate their children in the faith themselves. Resources for this are available from your nearest Catholic bookshop or online, for example:

- Redemptorist Publications: **www.rpbooks.co.uk/**

- Matthew James Publishing: **matthewjamespublishing.com/**

- Pauline Books and Media: **www.paulineuk.org/**

- St Paul's: **stpauls.org.uk/**

- Catholic Truth Society: **www.ctsbooks.org**

There are also many websites for Catholic parents to obtain resources for home learning.

You can also ask your parish priest and/or parish catechist for advice as to what materials to use and where you can get them.

Sending your children to a Catholic school is a great help with their education and formation. Educating young people today is no easy matter in a society where everything needs to be instantly available and if you don't like it, you can either ignore it or throw it away. The Church is challenging educators today to ask themselves what kind of education we need to give our children, especially as the majority of these children will live to see the next century. Goodness knows what life will look like then! This is why Pope Francis and many others in education are asking:

Above all, the question is: how should we educate? What tradition do we have today to pass on to our children?

General Audience, 20 May 2015

Clearly it is not enough simply to leave it to the school. What is needed is a reawakening of a model of education and formation that recognises that one of the greatest ways to educate is through witness. Adults demonstrate the importance of Christian beliefs and values by living and putting them into practice every day – and that means adults at home, in school and in the parish. Pope Francis warns us to take care never to:

sell off the human and Christian values which testify as to the value of the family, the school and society.

Address to the Association of Catholic School Parents, Rome, 5 December 2015

Education is a holistic endeavour, which seeks to form all parts of the human person not just for themselves but for the good of all God's people whatever their background, faith or culture.

Can. 795 *Education must pay regard to the formation of the whole person, so that all may attain their eternal destiny and at the same time promote the common good of society. Children and young persons are therefore to be cared for in such a way that their physical, moral and intellectual talents may develop in a harmonious manner, so that they may attain a greater sense of responsibility and a right use of freedom, and be formed to take an active part in social life.*

When considering the right school for your child it is important to talk as a family about what it is you want for this child. This brings us right back to the question of the meaning and purpose of education.

You cannot speak of Catholic education without speaking about humanity, because the Catholic identity is precisely that God became man.

Pope Francis, Address to World Congress on Catholic Education, Rome, November 2015

All Catholic schools are called to be Christ-centred in everything they do. Christ works in and through each person. The sanctity of life is based on the belief that your child is made in the image and likeness of God – a gift to you to love and cherish as your heavenly Father loves and cherishes you. Christ came in human form to show us how to love one another as one people, one body – the body of Christ, to live in communion with each other. Christ came as a brother for all. We are now called to show to the world how to be brothers and sisters to each other. We are one family; God's family.

> [The Church's] mission is to bring to all a love which cannot remain silent. The Church follows Jesus Christ along the paths that lead to every man and woman, to the very ends of the earth. In each of our neighbours, then, we must see a brother or sister for whom Christ died and rose again. What we ourselves have received, we have received for them as well. Similarly, all that our brothers and sisters possess is a gift for the Church and for all humanity.
>
> Pope Francis, Message for Lent 2015, 27 January 2015

What do governors expect of parents?

In the fast-changing world of education the introduction of academies now means that some schools also operate with an overarching board of directors. However, all directors and governors are still accountable to their local bishop.

Governors are the unsung heroes and heroines of the education system.

It is important for parents to recognise that governors give their time and expertise voluntarily. They are not paid for the work they do. Many governors give an extraordinary amount of time to the school and at the end of the day they are held responsible for the school in the name of the bishop. Governors know only too well that the education and needs of the children come first. Nothing must get in the way of that mission. It is important that governors are familiar with the life of the school and hear first-hand from you, the parents, about what you feel is going well and what may need to improve.

How should parents get in touch with governors?

Parent consultation evenings are a good opportunity to meet governors. It is unlikely that all the governors will be there, but some will and they want to hear from you.

Becoming a governor

School governors are always in short supply. Let your parish priest know if you are interested in finding out more about being a governor or contact your diocesan education office directly. If you are a practising Catholic then you have the possibility of becoming a foundation governor.

Parent–teacher associations (PTAs)

This is a popular area for parents to really get involved in a wide range of social and fundraising activities for their school. This is not as time-consuming as being a governor, but it is an essential aspect of any school. Activities such as the school fair, trips out, fun days all need an extra pair of hands.

Friends of the school

Another version of the PTA is the less formal process of having a Friends of the School Association. They are quite simply "friends" of the school who would like to offer their services and support. They do not have to be parents and the membership is open to anyone who would like to support the school.

Building fund

Families of children at all voluntary aided (VA) schools will be asked to make a voluntary contribution each year to the diocesan building fund. As a VA school, governors must find ways to fund 10% of all capital works (building projects and school improvements). This is very difficult for schools because they know how difficult this can be for some families. The governors are in a dilemma here. If they can't raise the 10% then there will be no building or improvement work on the school. Some schools rely heavily on support from special collections from their parishes to help with building works. This is fine if the parish has a large Mass attendance. Many, however, are struggling to pay parish costs, so may find it difficult to take on school building works as well. Parishioners also feel that those parents who do not contribute to the parish collection should be invited to do so. Governors and PTAs will run fundraising events, but they will also ask parents to make a voluntary contribution. If you have more than one child in the school you will notice that this is taken into account and a sliding scale is in place to help. However, if it is not possible to pay then the school fully understands and hopefully you will not be pressured or embarrassed. (Academies are 100% government funded, which exempts them from finding the 10% contribution.)

What does the school expect of parents?

The school relies very heavily on parental support for the formation in the faith of their children. One of the biggest challenges facing Catholic schools today is the double life that children, particularly in primary school, sometimes find themselves in. By this I mean one set of beliefs and values at school and another at home. Children very quickly see through what adults say and soon decide whether or not the adults really believe in what they are asking of their children. Teachers depend on parents working with them and the school reinforcing what is important in the home.

Prayer and worship are part of the everyday life of all Catholic schools. Therefore this needs to be part of family life as well; so too the receiving of the sacraments, particularly attendance at Sunday Mass and regular confession. Many Catholic schools have a voluntary Mass and will celebrate high moments in the school year with a special celebration. However, this does not replace parental responsibility for attendance at Sunday Mass.

It is wonderful when a child in class talks about how the family prays together and talks about their faith. This is the greatest support you can give your child's faith development – the family taking it seriously. This does not mean that parents won't encounter the often turbulent and difficult teenage years. But allowing honest and open discussion helps the young person explore her or his beliefs and values.

Teenage doubts and uncertainties

It is the role of the school to help young people develop enquiring and critical minds. Their teachers are there to challenge them to think deeply and grapple with the really difficult questions of their lives in the twenty-first century. This can sometimes be very difficult for parents who don't understand why their child appears to be so unaccepting of religion, faith and the need for any of it. First of all, this is not untypical and in fact is part of the maturing process. Young people want to discover the truth for themselves. This is what their school is trying to help them to do. It is not uncommon for a family to send a young person round to the convent, having given up on trying to debate an issue with their teenager. I always find young people exciting and interesting. It is great news that they are thinking for themselves. How to lead them to explore their ideas about God and the Church is the real art. One thing that doesn't work is the old dogmatic approach, which says, "You believe and do what I tell you!" What we all have to remember is that faith is a gift from God. However hard one tries you can't give anyone faith or make them believe. It is a gift freely given and freely received. It can also be taken from us!

The best teachers will always challenge young people to be able to justify their beliefs and values so that once they leave school they will be able to hold their own on firm ground and not be buffeted about by every prevailing opinion of the time.

Support your child's learning

Teachers will need your help in supporting your child's learning at all stages of their school life. Primary children will bring home reading books on a regular basis. You can make a considerable difference to their progress by just giving twenty minutes a night to hearing them read. So too with all their other learning. If possible sit with the younger children and help them with any homework. It is very difficult for a young child to just "get on with it".

Schools often ask parents to come and help with listening to children read, support school-based projects and share their work experiences. Grandparents and great-grandparents provide wonderful learning experiences from the past. Children love to hear about the past and personal stories.

Secondary-age pupils are a different kettle of fish! Yes, they are more able to work alone, but they too need your interest and help. Talk to them about their classwork and homework. Get them to share some of it with you. You always know the parents who do this because the quality of the students' work is much higher when parents are checking it. Checking does not mean asking, "Have you done your homework?" because nine times out of ten the child will simply say "yes" or "it's not due yet". Looking at your children's work in their books is very revealing. If you are not satisfied with the quality and standard of the work, challenge the young person to do it again and add a parental comment in the book for the teacher.

If you notice a lack of marking then send a message to the school. Most teenagers hate any fuss! So contact the school independently or phone the pupil's head of year and politely enquire as to why the book has not been marked. It may well be that it has not been handed in.

Close communication

Schools are delighted to hear from parents and welcome contact with all parents and carers.

It is very important to have at least one adult from your child's family at consultation evenings/parents' nights. This can be difficult for some families but if a parent can't come, then perhaps another adult member of the family might be able to attend. It is very disheartening for pupils of all ages if they have no one who will attend these meetings. If the date arranged for parent consultation presents problems then make another time with the school when you could go and meet with the tutor or head of year.

Supporting the learning in the school

The expectations on teachers today are enormous. In fact it is quite impossible to get through the required tasks for each day without extra help. This is very evident in primary schools where parents and grandparents often come into school to hear children read and help with activities.

In both primary and secondary schools parents are invited in to help the children understand the world of work. Here they can give an overview of what a particular profession is all about. The most popular are always visits from those doing what young people consider to be the "exciting jobs", like firefighters – even better if they are accompanied by the fire engine – or working for the police, especially dog handlers if the dog comes too. So too for authors and artists – pupils of all ages love stories and to meet an author, artist or musician is very special.

Getting to know other faiths

If you are a parent of another faith or denomination and would be willing to come into school to talk about your faith and what it means to you then you are like "gold" to a teacher. It is much better to hear from someone who is part of a faith group than to talk about it from an outsider perspective. The pupils will ask interesting questions and these are usually much better answered from a member of that faith group.

Celebrating the global Catholic family

Many Catholic schools now have "One World" celebrations where the pupils' families are invited to wear their traditional dress, and provide entertainment through music, dance and food from their countries. This is a wonderful opportunity for all families to share the richness and diversity of the school community.

What do young people hope for?

Generally young people want to do well in school and they need to know that their parents are proud of them. They are delighted when a message has gone home letting the parents know some good news about them. Many secondary schools encourage the pupils to attend consultation evenings with their parents. This can either be an awful ordeal or a really affirming encouragement.

Parental support and encouragement are essential. It is not easy for pupils today with so much pressure and the constant testing of children that is required by government. It is quite heartbreaking to hear eleven-year-olds say that their greatest wish at the end of their primary school is to be a Level 5 or 6! It is a sad indictment of our educational system that this appears to be the only measure of success and happiness. Of course the school will encourage and help each child to reach the highest possible academic standards, but there is so much more to each young person that cannot be measured and categorised by a level indicator.

Secondary students are also under great pressure, especially as the curriculum becomes ever narrower and the opportunities to develop individual gifts and talents seem to be shrinking by the year.

One of the most important things for all young people is that they are loved and valued for who they are. Young people are quick to pick up the spoken and unspoken wishes of their parents and this can sometimes translate into a feeling of not being good

enough. So often I have said to anxious parents that their child is doing his or her best and that is fine. Of course, when it is a case of laziness or underachievement then that is another matter. Not everyone learns or matures in the same way. For some study and learning come naturally and often these young people are highly motivated. For others they will take time to find the motivation to really excel. I always admire those parents who instil in their children that they will do all they can to help them find their place in life and be who they are created to be. Very often it is those students who are supported and encouraged rather than being pressurised that excel.

As challenging as young people can be, they long for support, understanding and patience. As the children grow into young adults they go through all the normal adolescent stages but they need frequent reminding that they are loved just as they are.

One of the greatest gifts you can give young people is to be there for them, listening and building up their confidence. It is very important that parents monitor their children's home activities to ensure that they do not become totally reliant on social media for friendships and relationships. The school will do much to try to develop social skills. Sadly this is all too easily undermined at home because parents are so busy or are not aware of what is really happening.

POINTS FOR FAMILY DISCUSSION

- ⚔ The Church takes seriously the role of parents as the first educators of their children. How do you feel about this?
- ⚔ Has this chapter identified ways in which you might further support your child's learning? Talk about this together.
- ⚔ As a family do you feel you listen to each other enough and help with learning? How might this be further improved?
- ⚔ Consider having a time each week when the family listens to one person talk about something new that he or she has learnt or done. Discuss this together.
- ⚔ Many schools are really keen to identify interesting stories about local people who have done or are doing something very interesting. Think about your family. This may not be paid work but something that you are involved in for the common good. Talk about this together and let the school know as they may well like you to be a speaker for a class.

 Reflection

Spend a few moments reflecting on two statements by Pope Francis:

> The perfect family doesn't exist, nor is there a perfect husband or a perfect wife, and let's not talk about the perfect mother-in-law! It's just us sinners… A healthy family life requires frequent use of three phrases: "May I?", "Thank you," and "I'm sorry" and never, never, never end the day without making peace.

Address to Engaged Couples Preparing for Marriage, Rome, 14 February 2014

> The family is where we are formed as people. Every family is a brick in the building of society.

@Pontifex, Twitter, 23 October 2014

PART II

CHAPTER 7

What does the Catholic Church say about education?

Understanding the vision and mission of the Church in education

As parents you want the very best school you can find for your child. Identifying just the right school can sometimes prove to be difficult. The best schools are well known and identified by Ofsted as being outstanding and naturally they are heavily oversubscribed. Catholic schools are, in the main, outperforming maintained schools nationally on many fronts. This is why they are so sought after and you may find that there will be many more applications than places in some schools.

Vision into mission – parents and schools working together

Today many parents, not to mention grandparents, are struggling to pass on the teaching of the Church in a meaningful way that connects with life in the twenty-first century. This is no easy task, but Pope Francis insists that together we must:

> *Find new ways to spread the word of God to every corner of the world.*
>
> Address to Cardinals, March 2013

What we are experiencing today is the need to translate the vision and mission of the Church into a new language, one our children and families can understand. It is rather like the challenge a musical director faces with a great opera. The words remain the same; what changes is the way in which the music is presented, so that it connects with the time and the place. The very best producers know just how to help their artists become one with their audience in such a way that every person present in the auditorium feels that he or she is the sole focus of this production.

Transformation of the person for the transformation of society

The mission of the Church in education is very challenging because it is about the transformation of the person for the transformation of society.

> *The function exercised by the school in society has no substitute; it is the most important institution that society has so far developed to respond to the right of each individual to an education and, therefore, to full personal development; it is one of the decisive elements in the structuring and the life of society itself.*
>
> Sacred Congregation for Catholic Education, *Lay Catholics in Schools: Witnesses to Faith*, 1982, 13

What does this mean in today's world? The Catholic Church exists for mission and not for itself. The priority of mission flows from the Second Vatican Council's Decree on the Church's Missionary Activity.

The church on earth is by its very nature missionary since, according to the plan of the Father, it has its origin in the mission of the Son and the Holy Spirit.

Ad Gentes 2

Our mission is the mission of God. Jesus continually teaches his followers that they are part of God's mission team:

As the Father has sent me, so I send you.

John 20:21

This mission, therefore, must be the Church's highest priority. Today we hear Pope Francis often emphasising the fact that the Church does not have a mission for itself; rather, mission has a Church. Everything the Church is and does must serve that mission. In order to fulfil this mandate Pope Francis calls on everyone in the Church to reach out to one another, especially to those who are poor and marginalised, who make up two-thirds of the world's population.

I prefer a Church which is bruised, hurting and dirty because it has been out on the streets, rather than a Church which is unhealthy from being confined and from clinging to its own security. I do not want a Church concerned with being at the centre and which then ends up by being caught up in a web of obsessions and procedures.

Evangelii Gaudium, "The Joy of the Gospel", 49

Responding to the big questions of purpose and meaning

The Catholic school exists to help every child discover:

- Where they come from

- Who they are

- Why they are here

- Where they are going.

In responding to those big questions one is often challenged with many others, especially those concerning local and global issues of justice such as the dignity of the human person, stewardship and care for the earth, poverty, homelessness, refugees and equality, to name just a few. The Catholic Church teaches very clearly that every person is made in the image and likeness of the creator God. God is their Father and therefore all people are family – because we have the same Father. We have been gifted to our parents because God believes that they have the potential to love, cherish and bring up this child as God would wish. In our society today not everyone will agree, but that is not the point. The challenge is to be credible witnesses to these truths. We see each other as brothers and sisters; we are one people – God's people; we are one race – the human race – and therefore one family. This is how our schools are called to see each person regardless of his or her creed, social background or ethnicity. Every person is totally unique and carries a gift that the world not only waits for but desperately needs.

The mission of the Church in schools – missionary disciples

Very simply it is to help young people find answers to the big questions of purpose and meaning and help them to make the right moral choices so that they can find their place in the world and make a difference. Each young person is created for something essential for the world. Only that person can give his or her gift. The Catholic school exists to help young people find this gift and acquire as much learning, skills and above all wisdom as possible.

Pope Francis constantly calls the whole Church to change its thinking and way of acting so that we become missionary disciples:

I dream of a "missionary option", that is, a missionary impulse capable of transforming everything, so that the Church's customs, ways of doing things, times and schedules, language and structures can be suitably channelled for the evangelization of today's world rather than for her self-preservation.

Evangelii Gaudium 27

Why such an emphasis on being "missionary disciples"?

Mission is a passion for Jesus and at the same time a passion for his people.

Pope Francis, Message for World Mission Day 2015

Pope Francis is speaking to the global Church and to the whole world. However,

> *Based on findings from a recent Win/Gallup poll, the findings of the survey carried out in 2015 revealed that, "The UK is among the least religious countries in the world. In a global ranking of 65 countries, the UK came six places from last, with 30% of the population calling themselves religious. While 53% of people said they were not religious, only 13% said they were a convinced atheist and the remainder did not know how to define themselves."*
>
> *The Guardian, 12 April 2015*

We certainly need "missionaries" who are prophetic risk-takers, ready to adapt their methods of communication when and where necessary.

Know the mission

No one with any sense would set out on a demanding mission without first equipping himself or herself with as much information, knowledge and understanding as possible. One needs to know what the challenge might entail. Sadly I meet many parents who have little understanding of the mission of Catholic schools or what is expected of them. For many their understanding relates back to their own personal experience of being at a Catholic school themselves. In some ways there will be much that is familiar but a great deal has changed, which often leaves some parents feeling out of their depth or confused. The governors and all the staff in the school strive to focus on Jesus Christ as the centre of the community because they are all engaged in carrying on his work building a world fit for God's children – your children.

For over 125 years the Catholic Church has been speaking about the importance of forming and educating young people for the good of society as a whole. The need to educate for transformation is nothing new. We are called by Jesus Christ not only to be transformed into the people God has envisioned us to be, but also to be so configured into Christ that we actually allow Christ to shine forth in us. That is why it is so important to know what the Church is saying and teaching about our mission, otherwise how can we proclaim it?

Catholic schools among the best in the country

Clearly Catholic schools are generally performing above national expectations and are a real success story, but their existence is based on something much bigger than academic achievement. Each year the Catholic Education Service for England and Wales publishes the data produced by Ofsted as to how well schools are doing at a national level.

The Church has long recognised that pupils must be educated to the highest possible academic standards as laid down by the law of the Church.

> **Can. 806 §2** *Those who are in charge of catholic schools are to ensure, under the supervision of the local Ordinary, that the instruction given in them is, in its academic standards, at least as distinguished as that in other schools in the region.*

As we have seen from the data for 2015 in the Introduction (p. 4 above) it is not only the academic standards that are high but the education of the whole child. Inclusion and the preferential option for those in the greatest need are also top priorities in the mission of the Church in education.

Parents' responsibility to seek the best possible education

Parents are encouraged to seek out the very best school for their children because they are their first educators. This is a responsibility that must not be abandoned.

> *The* role of parents in education *is of such importance that it is almost impossible to provide an adequate substitute. The right and the duty of parents to educate their children are primordial and inalienable.*
>
> *Catechism of the Catholic Church*, 2221

Parents can sometimes feel at a loss as to how to support their children's education, let alone their education in the faith. So much seems to have changed. Parents frequently say, "It's not like when we were growing up." Maybe not. But that does not alter the fact that it is what the children see you actually putting into practice that forms a critical part of their education. Pope Francis has made just this point in speaking about parents, warning:

> *They tend to entrust [their children] more and more to the "experts", even in the most delicate and personal aspects of their lives, putting themselves alone in a corner; and thus parents today run the risk of excluding themselves from the lives of their children. And this is very grave!*
>
> General Audience, 20 May 2015

The school is there to support you in your children's education, encouraging the closest possible collaboration as the school builds on the learning that begins in the home.

> **Can. 796 §2** *There must be the closest cooperation between parents and the teachers to whom they entrust their children to be educated. In fulfilling their task, teachers are to collaborate closely with the parents and willingly listen to them; associations and meetings of parents are to be set up and held in high esteem.*

Why does the Catholic Church have schools?

The Catholic Church has long recognised the importance of education at all levels. In 1995, Cardinal Basil Hume said:

> *The purpose of education is to develop integrated human beings... The task of the Church in education can rarely have been more urgent or more difficult. It is also one of the most vital contributions the Church can make to the renewal of our cultural and social life.*
>
> Speech to Catholic Head Teachers, Westminster, 1995

As Pope Francis says:

To help children, young people and adults to know and love the Lord more and more is one of the most exciting aspects of education. It builds up the Church!

Address to International Catechetical Congress, 27 September 2013

Passing on the faith is critical to the mission of the Church in education. It goes further than simply providing an excellent academic education. Catholic schools exist:

to form men and women who will be ready to take their place in society, preparing them in such a way that they will make the kind of social commitment which will enable them to work for the improvement of social structures, making these structures more conformed to the principles of the Gospel.

Sacred Congregation for Catholic Education,
Lay Catholics in Schools: Witnesses to Faith, 1982, 19

Catholic education seeks to educate all pupils so that wherever they see injustice or lack of respect for the person they are able to challenge, know how to work for change and in so doing continue the process of transformation for the common good of all.

The vision of the Church in education is driven not by a book, document or policy but by the person of Jesus Christ, the one who was called "Teacher". There are ninety recorded occasions in the Gospels when Jesus is spoken to directly. Interestingly, on sixty of these occasions he is addressed as "Teacher"

by both the crowds and the disciples. The title is affirmed by Jesus himself when he says, "You call me Teacher and Lord – and you are right, for that is what I am" (John 13:13). Nicodemus, a highly respected Pharisee and member of the Sanhedrin, comes secretly to Jesus at night for fear of being spotted and says, "We know that you are a teacher who has come from God" (John 3:2). Jesus' teaching was and still is immensely powerful, as the Scottish theologian James Stuart says:

The teaching of Jesus has had a power and an effect with which the influence of no other teacher can even for a moment be compared.[1]

1 As quoted in "Lessons from the Master Teacher", Keep Believing Ministries <http://www.keepbelieving.com/articles/lessons-from-the-master-teacher/> accessed 14 March 2016.

This lovely poem by an unknown author sums it up perfectly for us today:

Jesus the Teacher

He never taught in a classroom.

He had no tools to work with, no whiteboards, maps or charts.

He used no subject outlines, kept no records, gave no grades, and his only text was ancient and well worn.

His students were the poor, the lame, the deaf, the blind, the outcast.

His method was the same with all who came to hear and learn. He opened eyes with faith…

He opened ears with simple truth. He opened hearts with love – a love borne of forgiveness.

A gentle man, a humble man, he asked and won no honours, no gold awards of tribute to his expertise or wisdom.

And yet, this quiet teacher from the hills of Galilee has fed the needs, fulfilled the hopes, and changed the lives of many millions.

For what he taught brought heaven to earth and God's heart to all people.

Christ at the centre

Christ, therefore, is the teaching centre, the model on whom the Christian shapes his or her life. This is very simple on the one hand and yet immensely challenging on the other.

Christ's love for us is freely given. We are free to accept or reject it. What won't change is God's unconditional love for us, which in Jesus Christ is not only unconditional but sacrificial. He gives everything that a person can give and then gives more, proving his love for all people. In the Creed we proclaim that he:

> *… suffered under Pontius Pilate,*
>
> *was crucified, died and was buried;*
>
> *he descended into hell;*
>
> *on the third day he rose again from the dead.*
>
> Apostles' Creed

Christ loves us that much! Christ sums up the whole of the Jewish Law in his summary of the commandments:

> *"You shall love the Lord your God with all your heart, and with all your soul, and with all your mind." This is the greatest and first commandment. And a second is like it: "You shall love your neighbour as yourself." On these two commandments hang all the law and the prophets.*
>
> Matthew 22:37-40

The challenge for us is how to keep this story alive in a way that people of today can really hear and understand in their homes and schools.

How can I find out about the Church's teaching on education?

The table in the Appendix on pp. 112-14 below will help you to see continuing themes from the Church on education, formation and transformation. The table begins in 1885 so that you can see the evolution in thinking and understanding, but also because it was in 1885 that Rome recognised the great lengths that the bishops of England and Wales were putting into trying to educate Catholic children. Great Britain gets a special mention!

In your country of Great Britain We know that, besides yourselves, very many of your nation are not a little anxious about religious education. They do not in all things agree with Us; nevertheless they see how important, for the sake both of society and of men individually, is the preservation of that Christian wisdom which your forefathers received through St Augustine, from Our Predecessor, Gregory the Great… As often as We think of this, so often are We deeply moved, for We love with a paternal charity that island which was not undeservedly called the Mother of Saints; and We see, in the disposition of mind of which We have spoken, the greatest hope and, as it were, a pledge of the welfare and prosperity of the British people.

Go on, therefore, Venerable Brethren, in making the young your chief care; press onward in every way your episcopal work; and cultivate with alacrity and hopefulness whatever good seeds you find: for God, Who is rich in mercy will give the increase.

Pope Leo XIII, *Spectata Fides* 5-6

It was not until 1965, in *Gravissimum Educationis*, the Declaration on Christian Education, that a more comprehensive outline of the Church's mission in education was articulated by the Second Vatican Council. Furthermore, the Council recognised that it would not have time to revise Canon Law and it was not until 1983 that what some call the final document of Vatican II, the *Code of Canon Law*, appeared. The main tenets of the Declaration now moved into church law, giving them an additional authority. The publication of *The Catholic School* in 1977 picked up and further developed much of the Declaration on Christian Education.

In the table in the Appendix on pp. 112-14 below are some of the key documents from the Church on Christian education spanning more than 125 years. Each document acknowledges the critical role of Catholic schools. Throughout, the message has constantly been the same. Catholic schools are essential to the mission of the Church. Over the years, as each challenge threatening Catholic schools has appeared, the Church has responded, constantly restating the right to educate her young people in the beliefs and values of who they are as God's children. The Church is once more inviting us to revisit her teaching about Catholic education as an urgent task.

The redefinition of Catholic schools' identity for the 21st century is an urgent task. Going back to the documents issued by the Congregation for Catholic Education can be quite helpful in this respect, together with the experience that has been made over time in Catholic teaching, both in diocesan and congregational schools.

Congregation for Catholic Education, "Educating Today and Tomorrow: A Renewing Passion", *Instrumentum laboris*, 2014, III

A renewing passion

The 2014 document "Educating Today and Tomorrow: A Renewing Passion" focuses on education today and for tomorrow. The pace of change is so great today that the Church recognises the need not just to keep up with change but to lead and be part of the formation of society today and in the future. Catholic education seeks to try to understand the world we live in, make sense of it and enable young people to have the confidence, skills and knowledge to be the transformers of society.

The challenge of Catholic social teaching for today

One of the great treasures of the Catholic Church is its social teaching. Sadly, this wealth of wisdom has for many decades been relatively unknown. It is in this area of teaching that we can further identify what is meant by the transformation of society and the responsibility of each person for justice in society today. With those who are poor and marginalised making up two-thirds of the world's population, education for justice cannot be an optional extra for those who are interested.

No one must say that they cannot be close to the poor because their own lifestyle demands more attention to other areas. This is an excuse commonly heard in academic, business or professional, and even ecclesial circles. While it is quite true that the essential vocation and mission of the lay faithful is to strive that earthly realities and all human activity may be transformed by the Gospel, none of us can think we are exempt from concern for the poor and for social justice.

Pope Francis, *Evangelii Gaudium* 201

An overview of some of the social justice themes in the teaching of the Church

Dignity of the human person

Every human person is created in the image and likeness of God. Therefore, every person's life and dignity must be respected and supported from conception until the end of his or her natural life on earth. An institution's worth must be assessed in how it threatens or enhances the life and dignity of the human person.

Family and community

The human person is not only sacred, but social. How society is organised, be it socially, economically, legally or politically, has a direct impact on the dignity and growth of every human person and community. All people have a right to work to support themselves and their families as well as building up the common good for all. With the many challenges and difficulties facing families today it is crucial that families feel supported and strengthened.

Solidarity and the common good

We are all the people of God, one family. Therefore what happens to one has an impact on all, locally, nationally and globally. At the heart of solidarity is the pursuit of peace and justice. Our love for all calls us to work for a peaceful and just society where everyone has a fair share of the goods needed for a sustainable life, and opportunities for growth and development are offered equally. The dignity of every person is respected.

Dignity of work

Work is a way in which we can continue to participate in God's creation. Work gives dignity to life and must be carried out in such a way that the basic rights of workers are respected. Everyone has the right to productive work, to fair wages, and to organise and join a union. The economy must be conducted so that it serves the needs of the people. It is a means to an end, not the end goal.

Rights and responsibilities

Every person has a fundamental right to life. It is this right that makes all other rights possible. Everyone has the right to food, health care, housing, education and employment. We all need to strive to secure and respect these rights for others both locally and globally.

Option for the poor and vulnerable

Society is judged on how it cares for and stands with those who are poor and vulnerable – our brothers and sisters. We read in scripture how God has a special concern for the oppressed, poor, vulnerable and those forced to the margins of society. The Church calls us to respond to the cry of those who are poor and put their needs first. This preferential option for poor and vulnerable people must be seen in action in our daily lives and government policies.

Stewardship

The world that God created has been entrusted to everyone and we are responsible and accountable to God as stewards of the earth. The world has been given to us as a gift, to enjoy and care for so that future generations can enjoy it too. It is in caring for creation that we show our love and respect for its creator.

Accessing Catholic social teaching – the main papal and Vatican documents

- *Rerum Novarum* (On the Condition of Labour) – Pope Leo XIII, 1891

- *Quadragesimo Anno* (After Forty Years) – Pope Pius XI, 1931

- *Mater et Magistra* (Christianity and Social Progress) – Pope John XXIII, 1961

- *Pacem in Terris* (Peace on Earth) – Pope John XXIII, 1963

- *Gaudium et Spes* (Pastoral Constitution on the Church in the Modern World) – Second Vatican Council, 1965

- *Dignitatis Humanae* (Declaration on Religious Freedom) – Second Vatican Council, 1965

- *Populorum Progressio* (On the Development of Peoples) – Pope Paul VI, 1967

- *Octogesima Adveniens* (A Call to Action) – Pope Paul VI, 1971

- *Evangelii Nuntiandi* (Evangelisation in the Modern World) – Pope Paul VI, 1975

- *Laborem Exercens* (On Human Work) – Pope John Paul II, 1981

- *Sollicitudo Rei Socialis* (On Social Concern) – Pope John Paul II, 1987

- *The Church and Racism: Towards a More Fraternal Society* – Pontifical Council for Justice and Peace, 1989

- *Centesimus Annus* (The Hundredth Year) – Pope John Paul II, 1991

- *Veritatis Splendor* (The Splendour of Truth) – Pope John Paul II, 1993

- *Evangelium Vitae* (The Gospel of Life) – Pope John Paul II, 1995

- *Dignitas Personae* (The Dignity of a Person) – Congregation for the Doctrine of the Faith, 1998

- *Ecclesia in America* (The Church in America) – Pope John Paul II, 1999

- *Fides et Ratio* (Faith and Reason) – Pope John Paul II, 1998

- *Doctrinal Note on Some Questions Regarding the Participation of Catholics in Political Life* – Congregation for the Doctrine of the Faith, 2002

- *Compendium of the Social Doctrine of the Church* – Pontifical Council for Justice and Peace, 2004

- *Deus Caritas Est* (God Is Love) – Pope Benedict XVI, 2005

- *Sacramentum Caritatis* (The Eucharist as the Source and Summit of the Church's Life and Mission) – Pope Benedict XVI, 2007 (especially paragraphs 47, 49, 82-84 and 88-92)

- *Caritas in Veritate* (Charity in Truth) – Pope Benedict XVI, 2009

- *Evangelii Gaudium* (The Joy of the Gospel) – Pope Francis, 2013

- *Laudato Si'* (On Care for our Common Home) – Pope Francis, 2015

While the list above comprises the main documents from Rome, bishops from many different countries have also written their own application of the Church's social teaching as it applies in their part of the world. A good example of this would be the 1996 publication by the Catholic Bishops' Conference of England and Wales entitled *The Common Good and the Catholic Church's Social Teaching*.

Cardinal Basil Hume, Archbishop of Westminster at the time of the document's publication, opens the document with the words:

> It is the task of bishops of the Church to preach and teach the Gospel; to point people in the direction of Christ… The Gospel imperative to love our neighbour entails not only that we should help those in need, but also address the causes of destitution and poverty. The deepening of the spiritual life must go hand in hand with practical concern for our neighbour, and thus with social action.

At the time this document caused quite an outcry in some quarters as it was both challenging and radical. The bishops were accused of "meddling in politics", but as Cardinal Hume pointed out:

> In every society respect for human dignity requires that, so far as possible, basic human needs are met. The systematic denial of compassion by individuals or public authorities can never be a morally justified political option. The Church does not present a political programme, still less a party political one.

The bishops then go on to point out that what is needed is a change of minds and hearts of all people – that is the agenda, which is far greater than any government alone can achieve because it is a spiritual revolution, not a political one, that is needed.

Shortly after the publication of *The Common Good* came a second document from the bishops, *The Common Good in Education*, which challenged all involved in Catholic education to review the quality of their authentic witness to the mission of the Church in education.

POINTS FOR FAMILY DISCUSSION

 What vision do you have of the role of the Catholic school for society today?

 What do you really want from a school for your child?

 Where do you prioritise the practice of faith in your life?

 How committed do you feel that you can be to support your child in all his or her learning?

 What support would you like in order to support your child in his or her faith journey?

Reflection

Christ our Lord, you give us our lives: all that we are, our bodies and our minds.

You inspire us to learn more about the world around us, about you, about ourselves and about one another.

May we who enjoy the freedoms that you give us rejoice in our discoveries and work tirelessly for education for all.

May those who take risks and make sacrifices for their own education or the education of others inspire us always in our pursuit of learning and the life of faith.

May we learn from one another, gain the knowledge to build a better world, and realise the potential you give to all.
Amen.

(Daniel Hale/CAFOD)

CHAPTER 8
Who is responsible for a Catholic school?

All schools who bear the title "Catholic" are responsible to the bishop of the diocese they reside in. It is not uncommon to discover that many people think that voluntary aided (VA) Catholic schools are governed by and responsible to the local authority in the same way that all other maintained schools are. Even some local education authority personnel sometimes make this mistake. Not to mention parents who get totally confused!

Why is the diocesan bishop responsible?

This is clearly explained on the Catholic Education Service (CES) website, where it is stated that:

> The diocesan bishop governs the particular Church entrusted to him as Vicar of Christ: he has proper, ordinary and immediate jurisdiction, exercised by him personally in Christ's name. Canon law provides that each diocesan bishop has strategic responsibility to commission sufficient school places to meet the needs of baptised Catholic children resident in his area.

> Christine Fischer, *Governance of a Catholic School: A Clarification of Roles and Responsibilities for England & Wales*, Catholic Education Service, September 2014

However, in densely populated areas this is often very challenging as the demand sometimes far outnumbers the available places. This is further compounded by the rapidly changing educational scene concerning the building of new schools.

How is the title "Catholic" attributed to a school?

Only the bishop can designate a school as being Catholic. This is defined for us in Canon Law.

Canon 803 §1 states that a school is Catholic if:

(a) It is controlled by a diocese or religious order (or other public juridical person);

or

(b) It is acknowledged in a written document as Catholic by the diocesan bishop.

The "control" specified in Canon 803 is normally established where the diocese or religious order owns the school and appoints the governing body (or at least a majority of it).

As we have seen in Chapter 7, Catholic schools operate as part of the mission of the Church and therefore they must be accountable and responsible to the person responsible for the Church in their diocese – the bishop – even those schools that are not in diocesan trusteeship but come under the jurisdiction of a religious order.

This means that the bishop is not only responsible for all Catholic schools in his diocese; he also has the duty to ensure that, as we have considered previously:

> **Can. 806 §2** *Those who are in charge of catholic schools are to ensure, under the supervision of the local Ordinary, that the instruction given in them is, in its academic standards, at least as outstanding as that in other schools in the region.*

The bishop must see that all Catholic schools are meeting this challenge. You will notice that the Church expects its schools to be of the highest possible academic standard. They must be at least outstanding. Even when Ofsted finds a school to be outstanding this does not mean that the school has "arrived". Not at all. It is very demanding to be performing at these high levels all the time and a school can easily slip. So the governors, head teacher and their leadership teams need to be ever vigilant that every child is getting the best possible education. Catholic schools are always striving for excellence, being the very best they can be. To this end the bishop will establish his own inspection service which will carry out what is known as a Section 48 inspection. He has the right to inspect a school at any time if he feels that there is a good reason to do so. Generally speaking, it is every five years for schools that are good or outstanding, but more often for those that are struggling with underperformance.

Who owns the Catholic school?

This can vary depending on the school and its history. However, most Catholic schools and the land they are built on are owned by the diocese or, in the case of order schools, the religious order or congregation. These buildings and the land are then held in a charitable trust appointed by the bishop or the religious order. Trustees are appointed by the bishop or order to ensure that they are managed, cared for and used for the purpose for which the trust was set up. Their governing documents are known as the Trust Deed.

The Trust Deed

This is a key legal document and from time to time you will hear representatives of the diocese or your parish priest referring to it. You may be surprised to discover that it actually says very little about schools but deals in the main with the management of finances, assets and the estate of the trustees. However, you will see a statement that refers to the "maintenance or advancement of the Roman Catholic religion". Some dioceses do have a short reference to schools but no more than a sentence or two. These brief statements provide the legal basis for all that is done in the name of Catholic education at every level. It is for this purpose that governors are appointed – the "advancement of the Roman Catholic religion". This seems a rather broad statement, but it is meant to be, because the whole of the educational project of the Church is about just this. Put into everyday language, it means proclaiming the Good News of Jesus Christ, and educating our young people in what this means for them today in accordance with the teachings of the Catholic Church.

The Instrument of Government

Every school/college has this document. It is very challenging and contains an important clause that outlines how the school must be run:

The school was founded by and is part of the Catholic Church. The school is to be conducted as a Catholic school in accordance with the Canon Law and teachings of the Catholic Church, and in accordance with the Trust Deed of (name of diocese or religious order/ congregation)… *and in particular:*

(a) religious education is to be in accordance with the teachings, doctrines, discipline and general and particular norms of the Catholic Church;

(b) religious worship is to be in accordance with the rites, practices, discipline and liturgical norms of the Catholic Church; and at all times the school is to serve as a witness to the Catholic faith of Our Lord Jesus Christ.

The first paragraph is quite straightforward and simply underlines the legal status of the school from both the statutory and canonical points of view.

Paragraph (a) makes it clear that the teaching of Religious Education must fulfil that which is laid down by the bishop. For our purposes that is outlined in the *Religious Education Curriculum Directory*. Few parents are aware of this very important document.

Paragraph (b) in its first sentence refers to a wide area under the heading of religious worship. This asks governors to ensure that staff are properly trained and equipped to know how to educate and enable children and young people to learn about worship, liturgy and prayer.

The final part of this second paragraph is the most challenging of all. Notice the language: "at all times" – not just in RE lessons or during assemblies, but in everything – "to serve as a witness to the Catholic faith of Our Lord Jesus Christ". This is not easy. It is, however, part of the Instrument of Government and not an optional extra for the more pious members of the school community. It is for everyone who is part of the school. The challenge is obvious, and responding to and living this out needs a good deal of help, guidance and support.

The appointment of foundation governors

You may well ask why we need foundation governors if we are all committed to the same cause. It is a very good question. Foundation governors must be practising Catholics who are fully committed to their faith in the Church and Jesus Christ. Having looked at the Instrument of Government above, you can see that the bishop needs to appoint enough people to be able to support the whole governing body as they strive to make this a reality in their school. It is a long journey! That is why foundation governors form the majority of members of the governing body, to carry out the mandate entrusted to them by the bishop and safeguard the mission.

As other members of the governing body are elected or appointed through different avenues, they may or may not be Catholic or secure in their commitment to Catholic teaching. Hence the careful appointment by the bishop (or, in the case of schools owned and run by religious orders, the appointed person for the order) of foundation governors is necessary to ensure the Catholic nature of the school. (Academies have a different structure; however, the responsibility to comply with the requirements for Catholic education is the same.) Usually all governors are very committed and wanting to get it right. Once the whole governing body comes together they work as one united body.

Are foundation governors more important than the rest of the governing body?

No. All governors share in this responsibility as a corporate body. The reason why there are a variety of avenues through which governors are appointed is to ensure that the governing body has a wide range of expertise and skills that can be called upon to govern the school. Only the Chair in exceptional circumstances can act alone without consulting the rest of the governing body beforehand. However, the Chair must discuss any such emergency measures as soon as possible with the rest of the governing body.

The ethos statement

The law as regards the duty of the governors to secure an ethos statement is found in the Instruments of Government in the School Standards and Framework Act 1998 Schedule 12, paragraph 1:1, section (g) ("where the school is a foundation or voluntary school which has a religious character").

All schools that have a religious character must have an ethos statement. This forms part of the Instrument of Government and is quoted above in the section "The Instrument of Government".

What do we mean by "ethos"?

This is one of the terms that many governors and teachers in Catholic schools find difficult to put into clear terms. The word "ethos" comes from a Greek word for custom or habit. Simply put it is a way of living, behaving and doing things by people who, though diverse, follow common values, beliefs and vision of life. A Catholic school's ethos is seen in the many ways in which this common set of beliefs, values and vision is put into action and witnessed to in daily life. The Catholic Education Service's book *Christ at the Centre* defines "ethos" in this way:

> A Catholic school's "ethos" may be understood to be the outward signs and experiences of the teachings of Christ and the Catholic Church in the totality of daily life in a Catholic school.[1]

Therefore everything we are and witness to has to be consistent with our commitment to the personal experience of the teachings of Christ and the Catholic Church in the daily life of the Catholic school.

The final statement in both the Instrument of Government and the ethos statement is, as we have already seen, extremely challenging:

> and at all times the school is to serve as a witness to the Catholic faith of Our Lord Jesus Christ.

---

1   Marcus Stock, *Christ at the Centre: Why the Church Provides Catholic Schools* (London: Catholic Truth Society, 2012), A6.

This can sometimes be where many people feel they fall short. It's not surprising, we all do. What is important to remember is that this is what we are striving for. Does this let us off the hook? Not at all, but it serves to recognise that when we are challenged or realise that we have failed, or made the wrong decision, we have to be ready and willing to acknowledge our failure, do something about it and then be committed to learning from this. We are all learning and it is never easy. The only real mistake is the one we don't learn from. Parents, teachers and governors must be encouraged by the words of Pope Francis, who is not afraid to admit to his failings:

I am a sinner. This is the most accurate definition. It is not a figure of speech, a literary genre. I am a sinner.

Interview with Fr Antonio Spadaro, August 2013

What else are governors accountable for?

As we have seen, governors, along with the head teacher and senior leadership team, have a crucial role in ensuring the school is successful in meeting the needs of all its pupils and achieving high standards (Education Act 2002). They are also to ensure the well-being of pupils at the school, promote community cohesion and work in close collaboration with parents and carers. All of these responsibilities are clearly outlined and developed in the *Governors' Handbook* (Department for Education, September 2014, 1.2):

In all types of schools, governing bodies should have a strong focus on three core strategic functions:

a. Ensuring clarity of vision, ethos and strategic direction;

b. Holding the head teacher to account for the educational performance of the school and its pupils; and

c. Overseeing the financial performance of the school and making sure its money is well spent.

Governors as employers

This is one of the most important responsibilities of the governing body. The *Code of Canon Law* instructs governors to look for teachers who are ready and able to support the mission of the Church in education. Governors in Catholic VA schools are the employers of the staff, both teaching and support staff. In Catholic multi-academy trusts, it is the board of the company which is the employer of the staff in schools in the trust. The governing body acts as a committee of the trust. The board usually delegates responsibility for the recruitment of staff to the local governing body but it can't delegate its statutory responsibilities as employer. A Memorandum of Understanding agreed between the Department for Education and the CES protects Catholic interests within the trust.

Some staff may be employed through a service agreement with an outside body. However, it is still the responsibility of governors to ensure that these staff are fit for purpose in a Catholic school because:

> Teachers must remember that it depends chiefly on them whether the Catholic school achieves its purposes.
>
> Gravissimum Educationis, Declaration on Christian Education (1965), 8

The role of the priest on the governing body

It is important for the parish priest to be part of the governing body of a school in his parish. However, due to the falling numbers of priests available to serve as governors, appointing priests to governing bodies is becoming increasingly difficult for the bishops. This is a serious situation as the priest has a particular role to play as a governor of the school, a role that is often both challenging for the priest and can lead him into difficult situations. Let's listen to Canon Tony McBride – Episcopal Vicar for Education, Diocese of Salford, and foundation governor for many years – outline how he sees the role of the priest as a governor.

Canon, how is the role of the priest any different from that of any other foundation governor?

The Catholic school is primarily part of the mission of evangelisation of the Church and so the bishop has prime responsibility for the education of Catholics in his diocese. The parish priest, in cooperation with assistant priests, parents and teachers, has responsibility for the Catholic education of children. Therefore you can see that immediately the priest has a very wide brief, which is enshrined in Canon Law. Canon 528 §1 stipulates the responsibilities of a parish priest in relation to Catholic education within his own parish in collaboration with the bishop and the Christian faithful:

> He is to have a special care for the catholic education of children and young people. With the collaboration of Christ's faithful, he is to make every effort to bring the gospel message to those also who have given up religious practice or who do not profess the true faith.

That particular part of Canon Law shows the relationship between the mission of the local parish and the mission of the school: to provide a Catholic education for the children and, through the work of education, call those who have ceased in the practice of their faith back to the full practice of their religion. That is why a Catholic school has a duty to accept all children who have been baptised in the Catholic Church and not just those whose parents go to Mass on Sunday.

I am glad to hear you say that the Catholic school is for every baptised Catholic, but I am not sure that all priests see it that way.

Yes, there are some practices that exclude children who come from non-Mass-going families, but I am not happy about that because God, as a loving Father, is never content to leave his children in ignorance nor to allow them to live in error. The work of the parish priest and those who have the responsibility of educating our children in Catholic schools needs to be imbued with a spirit of cooperation and co-responsibility. The charism of being able to work together for the good of all must be alive in those responsible for the Catholic education of children.

The parish priest and assistant priest are automatically the chaplains to any Catholic school within the parish in which they have been appointed by the bishop to serve as priests. As such they are there to safeguard the teaching of the faith and to be a mentor and support to pupils and staff alike in the ways of faith. This is why in the Diocese of Salford we do not want parish priests to be Chairs of governors in their parish schools. Their responsibilities as priests go beyond the governance and management of our schools, although they are normally part of the governing body as foundation governors.

Conflicting roles

The point that Canon McBride is making about parish priests not being the Chair of governors is very important because the priest must be in a position to pastorally support all his parishioners without prejudice or favour. Parents and staff of the school must be able to feel that their priest is there for them.

He may not agree with a particular point of view, but he must support and guide everyone equally. So often parents will go to the parish priest if they can't get a place in their local Catholic school, or if there is a dispute of any kind involving the school. The priest must not take sides but work with the parents and others involved to find the best way forward.

Parent governors

As we saw in Chapter 2, Peter Jackson was a parent governor of his children's primary school for six years. This is a role you might like to consider. Most dioceses are very short of people who will volunteer to be governors. Peter, as he says, is not a Catholic, but this did not prevent him from standing for election as a parent governor. You can see from what he says that he has a very good understanding and deep commitment to his children's Catholic education. If there is a vacancy for a parent governor then perhaps you might like to find out more about being a governor and talk to your parish priest about it. Further information is available in my book entitled *How to Survive as a Governor in a Catholic School* (Chawton: Redemptorist Publications, 2015).

What access can parents have to the governing body?

It is really important that parents know who the governors are. This information is on the school website and often displayed somewhere near the main entrance. However, it is important for everyone to be clear about the role of parent governors. They are not there to represent parent views in terms of being the person that parents go to as an individual. Governing bodies are made up of a wide range of people who bring particular experience, knowledge, skills and wisdom to the body as a whole. Once elected, the parent governor becomes part of a team. Governors may not act alone on an individual basis but always as one – the governing body.

The CES gives good guidance on the requirement of governing bodies regarding elections of parent governors. It is the responsibility of the governing body to hold elections for these positions. The numbers of parent governors are laid out in the Instrument of Government of the school.

By virtue of Regulation 18 of the School Governance (Constitution) (England) Regulations 2007, SI 2007/957, each voluntary aided school must have at least 2 foundation governors who are eligible for election or appointment as parent governors. (A parent is eligible for election or appointment if he is a parent of a child at the school, a parent of a former pupil, or a parent of a child at or below compulsory school age.) For this reason, there will be fewer positions for elected parents than on the governing body of community or foundation schools of similar size and character.

CES guidelines, quoted at **www.rcdow.org.uk/**

What is the relationship between the local authority and a Catholic school?

That depends very much on the type of Catholic school. VA Catholic schools and academies have in many respects the same accountability to the local authority or Department for Education and Welsh Government as community schools. For example, academies must follow the same rules on special educational needs and exclusions as other state schools. They must provide a curriculum that is "balanced and broadly based, and includes English, mathematics and science".[2] As far as pupil admissions are concerned, academies still have to follow the same rules as maintained VA schools.

What about academies?

This is a fast-changing scenario and one that leaves many parents bewildered about what is going on. In October 2015, Prime Minister David Cameron announced he wanted "every school an academy" and "local authorities running schools a thing of the past". In November 2015 in the Government's autumn statement an official document stated that the next step towards the Government's goal of ending the local authorities' role in running schools was by all schools becoming academies. Many parents wonder where this leaves the governance of Catholic schools. While the picture is forever changing, governing bodies and academy boards of trustees of Catholic schools, whatever their status, remain under the guidance of the local bishop and are accountable to him.

---

2   Quoted at <fullfact.org/education/academies-and-maintained-schools-what-do-we-know/> accessed 16 March 2016.

What about other agencies?

Schools call on a wide range of supporting agencies and they are free to select the appropriate one for their needs and decide who can deliver the best service in line with the mission of the school. Head teachers have to be careful because some agencies may promote a line of thinking that is not acceptable.

How does the diocese support its schools?

All dioceses have support for schools through their diocesan websites. There you will find the contact details for the director of education/schools and the education team. In some dioceses this is quite extensive and covers every aspect of school life. Unfortunately some dioceses are not in the position to afford such a large team. However, there will be someone to talk to and signpost where you can get help.

Who funds Catholic schools?

The school buildings and the land on which Catholic schools are built are owned by the Catholic Church (or religious order). The Church provides these premises, at no charge, to enable the State to fulfil its obligation to provide education for the population. The day-to-day running costs of Catholic schools are funded by the state in the same way that all schools are funded (either through local authority or Department for Education funding agreements). The Church covers 10% of the capital costs for the maintenance of the premises, except in Catholic academies, which do not have to fund 10% of any capital grants or associated VAT. They get the full grant and claim back the VAT.

Academies are fully funded by the government.

Free schools are funded by the government but aren't run by the local authority. They have more control over how they do things.

Independent or private Catholic schools are free from local authority control because they are privately owned and do not have government funding.

What about free schools?

At the point of writing there are no Catholic free schools because of the Government's cap on 50% Catholic intake. Paul Barber, Director of the CES, said:

> Catholic schools are some of the best performing educational institutions in the country and there is a significant demand from parents. We are not opposed at all to the principle of free schools, however today's announcement will be disappointing news to the thousands of parents who are unable to get their child a place at a Catholic school. If it is a question of diversity and promoting community cohesion, it would be worth the Government remembering that 36% of pupils at Catholic schools come from ethnic minority backgrounds, six per cent higher than the national average. [3]

3   "CES Responds to Government's Free School Announcement", Catholic Education Service website <www.catholiceducation.org.uk/news/ces-news/item/1003011-ces-responds-to-government-free-school-announcement> accessed 16 March 2016.

The authority of the bishop

No authority body can replace the authority of the bishop over his schools. They can and do make recommendations and together with the bishop will find a way forward. However, at the end of the day it is the bishop who has the final say, in consultation with the governors, in any big or serious decisions concerning a Catholic school. The Section 48 inspection of schools by the bishop's inspectorate is another means of ensuring a high level of accountability. This partnership with the local authority is something that is greatly valued by the majority of schools. The demise of the local authority support for schools is something that many regret.

POINTS FOR FAMILY DISCUSSION

- Talk together about the bishop's responsibility for Catholic schools. Did you realise that he had so much responsibility? How do you feel about this?
- In what ways do you think a child attending a Catholic school who is not from a practising Catholic family might be helped?
- How do you see your responsibility of witnessing to Catholic beliefs and values?
- Catholic schools are among the best-performing schools in the country but they recognise that without the support of the family it becomes very difficult. Would you agree or disagree? Why?
- Find out who the parent governors are and talk to them about their roles. Would you consider standing for the position of parent governor or a foundation governor?

 Reflection

Life is an opportunity, benefit from it.
Life is beauty, admire it.
Life is a dream, realise it.
Life is a challenge, meet it.
Life is a duty, complete it.
Life is a game, play it.
Life is a promise, fulfil it.
Life is sorrow, overcome it.
Life is a song, sing it.
Life is a struggle, accept it.
Life is a tragedy, confront it.
Life is an adventure, dare it.
Life is luck, make it.
Life is too precious, do not destroy it.
Life is life, fight for it.

(Poem found on Mother Teresa's bedroom wall. Original source unknown)

APPENDIX

Key documents concerning worldwide Catholic education

Date	Document	Author	Key Concepts
1885	*Spectata Fides* On Christian Education	Pope Leo XIII	Importance of providing Catholic education for all Education and care for the young – "for the future condition of the state depends on the early training of its children"
1905	*Acerbo Nimis* Encyclical on Teaching Christian Doctrine	Pope Pius X	Importance of Christian doctrine as a means to combat religious ignorance
1929	*Divini Illius Magistri* Encyclical on Christian Education	Pope Pius XI	The educational environment defined as family, church, school Supreme importance of Christian education
1965	*Gravissimum Educationis* Declaration on Christian Education	Second Vatican Council	The right of all Christians to a Christian education Mission of the Church in education The importance of schools Duties and rights of parents Different types of Catholic schools
1972	*To Teach as Jesus Did: A Pastoral Message on Catholic Education*	US Conference of Catholic Bishops	Christian message, community and service Mission of the Church The need for planning and collaboration in developing educational programmes
1977	*The Catholic School*	Sacred Congregation for Catholic Education	The Catholic School and the saving mission of the Church Centre for human formation Integration of faith, life and culture Catholic schools, service to the Church, society and mission countries

Date	Document	Author	Key Concepts
1982	*Lay Catholics in Schools: Witnesses to Faith*	Sacred Congregation for Catholic Education	The role of lay educator in a Catholic school Synthesis of faith, culture and life Vocation rather than profession Witnesses to faith
1988	*The Religious Dimension of Education in a Catholic School*	Congregation for Catholic Education	Youth in a changing world The Catholic school is an open community Faith, life and culture Teaching of Religious Education The Christian formation process
1997	*The Catholic School on the Threshold of the Third Millennium*	Congregation for Catholic Education	Joys and difficulties Educating the human person The Catholic school at the heart of the Church Identity of the Catholic school The Catholic school at the service of the community
2002	*Consecrated Persons and Their Mission in Schools: Reflections and Guidelines*	Congregation for Catholic Education	Christ the teacher Radical response Church in communion – interface with the world Educators called to evangelise, accompany the young in a search for meaning Life as vocation The dignity of women – intercultural education Solidarity with the poor Culture of peace
2007	*Educating Together in Catholic Schools: A Shared Mission between Consecrated Persons and the Lay Faithful*	Congregation for Catholic Education	Communion in the mission of education Formation for educating together Communion for opening oneself towards others

Date	Document	Author	Key Concepts
2013	*Educating to Intercultural Dialogue in Catholic Schools: Living in Harmony for a Civilization of Love*	Congregation for Catholic Education	Culture in a plural society Culture and religion Approaches to pluralism Guidance for an intercultural approach Catholic education and intercultural dialogue The contribution and responsibility of Catholic schools
2014	*Educating Today and Tomorrow: A Renewing Passion* *Instrumentum laboris*	Congregation for Catholic Education (for Educational Institutions)	What kind of Catholic schools and universities? Current and future challenges